Daring to Stand Alone

Daring to Stand Alone

AN ENTREPRENEUR'S JOURNEY

J.W. Rinzler

in collaboration with
Delia Viader *&* Richard Mendelson

Book design by Suzi Hutsell

CAMERON + COMPANY
Petaluma, California

Dedicated to my father, Eng. Walter Viader

And How Long?

How long does a man live, after all?
Does he live a thousand days, or one only?
A week, or several centuries?
How long does a man spend dying?
What does it mean to say "for ever"?
. . .

—Pablo Neruda

Contents

Prelude

FIRE! THE THOUGHT SCREAMED in her head. The blonde, svelte woman had just arrived for an elegant dinner at the Meadowood Resort in Napa Valley. She was the honored guest of executives from Silicon Valley Bank. Her esteemed wines were the toast of the world. She had defied the odds. She'd raised four children by herself; had tirelessly traveled the world to promote the product of her hillside vineyards; had planted, tunneled, and built a fantastic winery and house.

Fire?! The voice coming through her phone was her son's; he was telling her the horrifying details. Her irreplaceable bottles, filled with the lifeblood of her winery, nurtured with love, dedication, and knowledge, were going up in smoke.

That October evening, Delia Viader had to think fast. She had to rely on her experience and self-discipline. After calmly telling her son that everything would be okay, she joined her dinner partners at their table, keeping her cool and biding her time. Later that evening she would inform the bankers matter-of-factly: "I'm going to need an extra million-dollar bridge-loan by year's end."

> *"I do believe that people can lead meaningful lives. We do have a purpose."*

They stared at her as she proceeded to tell them the reasons behind her request. But even if Delia did obtain the money before winter, there were no guarantees. Despite all of her meticulous hard work and the twenty years it had taken to place her unique bottles on the wine lists of the best restaurants throughout the world, she could still very well falter, fall off the map, be eliminated in an ultracompetitive industry because her stock was burning up in violent flames. Gone. Irreplaceable. Finished. Only time and her ability to pull herself back from the abyss would make the difference.

Delia had done it before . . .

PAGE 4: Delia and her father, Walter, on April 12, 2005. • LEFT: Delia Viader stands in her Napa Valley vineyard in 1994. This vineyard, which she built from the ground up over the previous decade, would go on to produce some of the best wines in the world in the years to follow.

A Compendious History of Napa Valley

THE FIRST VINES PLANTED in California date as far back as the late 1700s, but most American wine from those early decades originated in New York, Virginia, Ohio, Missouri, and Southern California. Some track the birth of Napa Valley wine to 1838, when George Yount, a native North Carolinian, planted his vineyard in what is today the town of Yountville, which was named after him. He was joined by other pioneers like Pennsylvania nurseryman Simpson Thompson, Massachusetts sea captain Joseph Osborne, and English brewmaster John Patchett. Some early pioneers, like Patchett, were initially attracted by the California Gold Rush and then settled in Napa Valley.

Many of Napa Valley's most historic wineries were founded by European immigrants in the latter half of the nineteenth century. Charles Krug from Prussia started Krug Winery in 1861 on land that he acquired as part of the dowry from his wife, Caroline Bale. German Jacob Schram purchased the property that today is Schramsberg Winery in 1862. Germans Jacob and Frederick Beringer started Beringer Brothers Winery in 1876. And Finnish sea captain Gustave Niebaum established Inglenook Winery in 1879. These and other European immigrants brought their winemaking know-how, their wealth, and their dreams to the valley.

The wine business in these early years was laboriously difficult and expensive. Glass bottles were pricey and hard to find. Wine was sold cheaply by the gallon. Vineyard pests were a problem. Despite the difficulties, wine production in America rose, particularly from the mid-1870s through the decade of the 1880s. In 1860, roughly 250,000 gallons of wine were produced in the state. That rose to 1.8 million gallons by 1870 and then skyrocketed to 14.6 million gallons by 1890.

During this same period, Northern California surpassed Southern California as the leading wine-producing region of the state, and Napa Valley established a reputation for high-quality wines. The two most famous Frenchmen in the Napa Valley were Jean Chaix and Jean Brun, who made their first wine in 1877. Their vineyards were on Howell Mountain, and their first winery was in Oakville, at what is today the Napa Wine Company. Brun and Chaix quickly realized the logistical problems of having a winery in Oakville and vineyards on Howell Mountain, especially when transport was by horse, so they decided to build a stone winery on Howell Mountain, the same area that Delia would choose. Later, another French couple, the former owners of La Mission Haut Brion in Bordeaux, would take over part of Brun and Chaix's winery and vineyards and rename it Château Woltner, which much later would change hands once again, be improved, and finally be renamed Ladera.

At the World Exposition in Paris in 1889, Napa Valley cemented its reputation on the world stage. Napa Valley wines won more medals than any other region in California or any other state. Of thirty-four awards won by Californian wine and brandy, Napa Valley collected twenty. Wine was booming in America, and Napa Valley was leading the way. In 1890, there were approximately 18,000 planted vine acres in Napa County, compared to around 3,600 vine acres in 1880.

European immigrants brought their winemaking know-how to the valley.

Unfortunately, the boom was followed by bust, caused by the twin scourges of phylloxera, a devastating root louse that killed vines around the world, and National Prohibition, which took effect in 1920. Prohibition ended the legal trade in wine and other alcoholic beverages in America, and many wine growers let their vineyards wither and die. Some survived by selling sacramental wines, which was one of the lawful exceptions to Prohibition. Prior to Prohibition, more than one thousand wineries were licensed in America. By 1933, when Prohibition was repealed, around 150 wineries remained in operation—130 in California and the rest in Ohio, New York, and other Eastern Seaboard states. The ensuing Depression didn't help either.

Following World War II, with a revived US economy, the tide started to turn. In 1944, a young Robert Michael Mondavi formed the Napa Valley Vintners Association with the help of six other vintners to "present a united front" and to "eat, drink, and be merry," in the words of cofounder Louis Martini. In 1947, they began another venture, the Napa Valley Wine Technical Group, to share the latest research and technological advances. Both groups remain active today.

Great progress was made to improve the quality of vineyards and wines, but the American consumer lagged behind until the 1970s. Author Leon Adams described that decade as the "American Wine Revolution." Wine consumption in America soared, increasing by 88 percent, from 236 million gallons in 1969 to 444 million gallons a decade later. Americans were also changing their taste for wine, from sweet and fortified wines to table wines—so named because they were usually served at the table with meals.

In Napa Valley, around forty-one new and refurbished wineries were established during the decade of the 1970s, increasing the total number of wineries to seventy-three. Over that same period, planted vine acres increased by 82 percent, from 12,254 to 22,261.

OLD WORLD VS. NEW WORLD

The popularity of Napa Valley wines specifically and California wines in general steadily grew. Consumers around the world were increasingly curious about these New World wines, so perhaps a head-to-head competition between the best wines of the New World and the Old World was inevitable. Who would win a "blind" test of French vs. US red and white wines from those countries' best wine regions?

Steven Spurrier, a British wine expert who owned a small wine shop, organized a competition. French judges carried out two blind tasting comparisons: one of top-quality Chardonnays from Burgundy and California and another of top-quality Cabernet Sauvignons from Bordeaux and California. The eleven judges were asked to grade each wine out of 20 points. No specific grading framework was given, leaving the judges free to grade according to their own criteria.

Without calling into question the abilities of the tasters, scientific concerns have been raised about the methodology used. Spurrier acknowledged in *Decanter* in August 1996 that he tallied the winners by "adding the judges' marks and dividing this by nine, which I was told later was statistically meaningless."

Although Spurrier had invited many reporters to the original 1976 tasting, the only one who attended was George Taber of *Time* magazine, who promptly reported the results to the world. Three of the four Bordeaux wines in the competition—Château Mouton Rothschild, Château Haut-Brion, and Château Montrose—were from the 1970 vintage, as was the entry from Heitz Cellar Martha's Vineyard (Napa Valley). The fourth Bordeaux wine, Château Léoville-Las Cases, as well as Ridge Monte Bello from Santa Cruz, were from the 1971 vintage. Freemark Abbey (Napa Valley) presented a 1969 Cabernet Sauvignon, and Clos Du Val (Napa Valley) unveiled its first release from the 1972 vintage. Stag's Leap Wine Cellars (Napa Valley) showed its 1973 vintage of S.L.V. The competition would become known as the "Judgment of Paris."

On May 24, 1976, to the shocking surprise of nearly everyone, three of the top four wines selected by the judges were from Napa Valley. The Sundance Film Festival of 2008 saw the debut of *Bottle Shock*, a feature film that dramatizes this 1976 wine tasting.

Three years later, another radical change took place in the Napa Valley. New World and Old World joined forces with the announcement that Robert Mondavi and Baron Philippe de Rothschild, owner of First Growth Château Mouton Rothschild, were forming a "joint venture" to create a single Bordeaux-style blend in Napa Valley aptly named Opus One. Their first jointly produced wine, a 1979 vintage, was released in 1984.

Throughout the 1980s, more intrepid entrepreneurs, including Delia, bought land in Napa Valley and began the laborious process of planting vines, making wine, and selling it. As we shall see later in this story, Delia's strong work ethic, her amiable personality, and her family values served her well as she established VIADER as one of Napa Valley's elite wines.

THE FRENCH PARADOX

In 1991, Delia and other vintners in Napa Valley and worldwide were aided tremendously by the phenomenon known as the French Paradox, referring to the classic *60 Minutes* story that aired in November of that year. The story opens with Morley Safer at a bistro in Lyon, ticking off fatty menu items—pig's head paté, black pudding, and other foods high in oil, butter, and animal fat. He then asks French scientist, Dr. Serge Renaud, the director of the nutrition and cardiology unit of the French National Institute of Health and Medical Research, how it is possible for the French to have lower levels of heart disease than Americans.

Renaud replies, "The farmers have been eating this for years. They've been eating a very high-fat diet, it seems, and yet they don't get heart disease." The answer, according to Renaud, lies in something else on Safer's café table: red wine.

With a glass in hand, Safer explained the emerging theory that red wine can flush fatty deposits, which cling to blood platelets on the artery wall, out of the body. "The answer to the riddle, the explanation of the paradox, may lie in this inviting glass," Safer said. With this one simple gesture, Morley Safer convinced Americans to drink more wine. While the French are also credited with eating more fresh food and far less processed foods than Americans, it was Renaud's verdict on red wine that really caught viewers' attention.

Renaud became a celebrity overnight. Born in Bordeaux, Renaud's grandfather owned a vineyard in Entre-Deux-Mers. Serge took his graduate degree in cardiovascular disease in Montreal before returning to France. "When I left France at the age of twenty to study in Canada, I couldn't imagine there was a population in the world that didn't drink wine with meals," he said. His time in Canada and his visits to America surprised him. He couldn't believe how rare wine was on American tables. "I was struck by the coronary heart disease rates in America, the dietary habits of Americans, and the absence of wine. After taking my doctorate in cardiovascular diseases in 1960, I decided to explore the relationship between nutrition and heart disease."

Three of the top four wines selected by the judges were from Napa Valley.

The French Paradox had a huge impact on American wine consumption. In the 1980s, US wine sales were growing, albeit slowly, and white wine was fashionable. By 1992, sales of red table wine in America increased by a whopping 39 percent, following a 4.5 percent decrease between 1980 and 1990, according to *Impact*, a sister publication of *Wine Spectator*.

Including a glass of red wine with a meal became the epitome of a healthy diet. The "Mediterranean" diet won the hearts and minds of the American public even though some suggest Renaud's findings were too simplistic. New studies continue to find health benefits from the moderate consumption of wine, even if those benefits are not fully understood. Once again, the stage was set for the wine business in Napa Valley to experience a quantum leap—and sure enough, the 1990s developed into what many consider to be the golden age of California wine.

This 1859 map of Napa Valley shows the epicenter of New World wine. The valley's rise to prominence in the mid-twentieth century saw it completely change the face of the global wine industry.

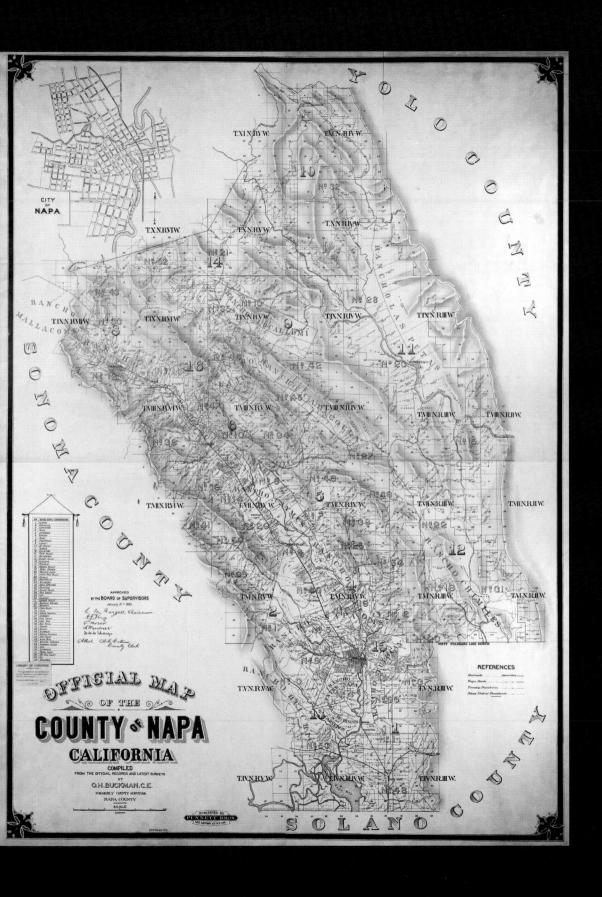

OFFICIAL MAP
OF THE
COUNTY OF NAPA
CALIFORNIA
COMPILED
FROM THE OFFICIAL RECORDS AND LATEST SURVEYS
BY
O.H. BUCKMAN, C.E.
FORMERLY COUNTY SURVEYOR
NAPA COUNTY
SCALE

CITY OF NAPA

YOLO COUNTY

SONOMA COUNTY

SOLANO COUNTY

REFERENCES

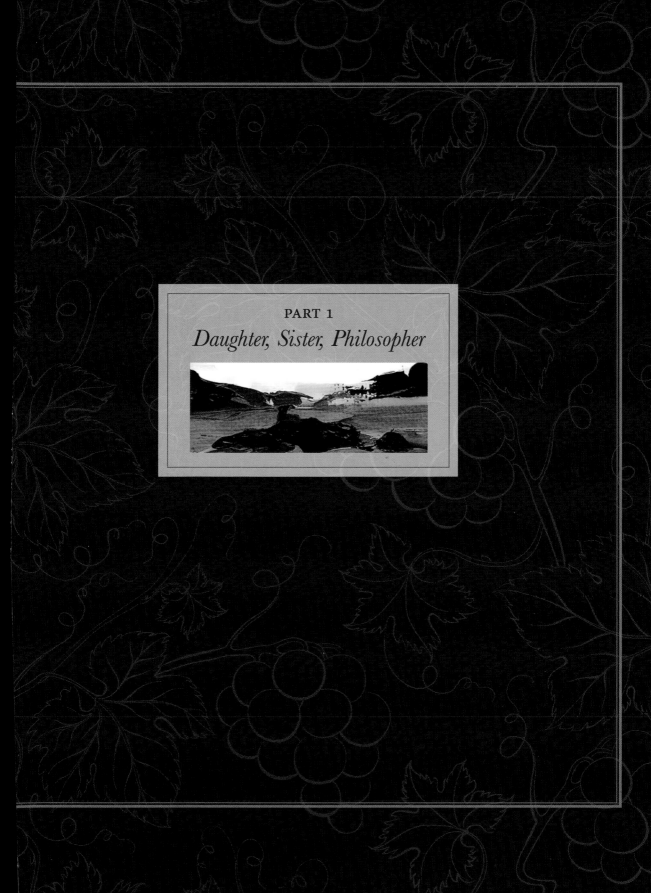

PART 1

Daughter, Sister, Philosopher

Free Spirit

DELIA EMILIA VIADER was born on April 12, 1958, at the British Hospital in Capital Federal, Buenos Aires, Argentina, which she refers to as "the Paris of South America." The Viader household was located in the Recoleta neighborhood, in the heart of downtown, though they also had several other residences—one in Hurlingham, forty minutes outside the capital, for quick weekend retreats; two built by the beach in Pinamar, for lazy summers at less than three hours' drive distance; and one "small" estancia, a cattle ranch of more than thirty-seven thousand acres south of the nearby city Coronel Suárez. Here, legendary asados—enormous barbecues of beef and various other meats cooked on a grill—were intertwined with polo matches for the family's entertainment.

Walter Viader, Delia's father, was an accomplished man: debonair, cool, with a passion for radio waves, the aerodynamics of rockets, and anything NASA-related. As a professional engineer in electronics, he first established a career in the military as a telecommunications advisor, then later as a diplomatic attaché. He traveled frequently and widely and was at times involved in tricky international negotiations concerning electrical, water, and nuclear resources, as well as matters of aerospace and turbines, tasks for which his calm demeanor was tailor-made.

Delia's mother, Delia Esviza, always accompanied her father, and hailing from a naval officer's family, she was well suited to the back-and-forth travel of the occupation. Indeed, she was born on the Marine base of Cowes, Isle of Wight, UK, but her sister Martha Alicia was born in Taranto, Italy, and their older sister Susana in Frankfurt, Germany. Although there was only a difference in age of ten years between her parents, Delia fondly recalls, "Dad could not start any story without referring to it in jest: 'When I married your mother, right after she graduated kindergarten . . .'"

Delia as a baby in Argentina. Born in 1958, she was Walter and Delia Viader's first child.

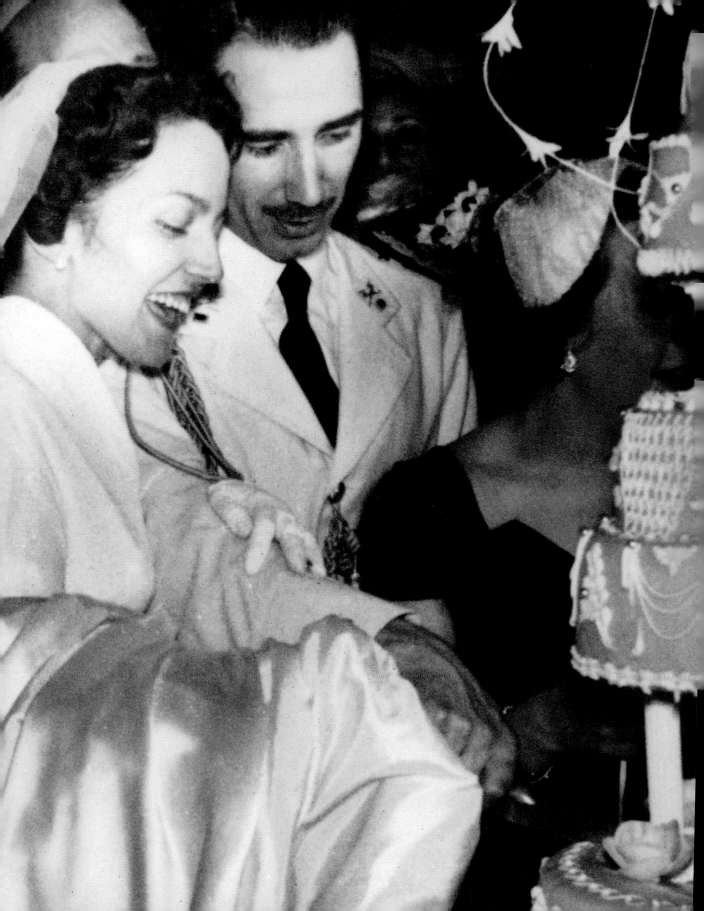

Delia's mother always worked outside the home, pursuing her own interests and never thinking for a moment that her main purpose was to be at home. As Delia puts it, "I don't think she would even enter the kitchen other than to make sure that the cook had done whatever she directed."

Delia, the eldest of three, was named after the Greek goddess Artemis, who was born on the island of Delos and sometimes referred to as Delia. While her mother would always refer to the origin of her name as a diminutive of Cordelia, as in the character of William Shakespeare's tragic play *King Lear*, Delia's father had his own name for her. "My father would affectionately call me 'little bug' or 'firefly'—*bichito de luz* . . . I was supposed to be a boy. Everybody bet on a boy, so I was dressed in blue for the first year of my life."

Next to come to the Viader family were two boys: Walter Jr., a year later, and Christian, five years Delia's junior. The three siblings remain very close, though her two brothers preferred to call her just "bug"—*bicho*—which, when they were growing up, "used to *bug* the hell out of me," she says.

"My father treated me the same as my two younger brothers," Delia adds. "From the very beginning, it was established that I was the first. I was the one to dictate what kind of game we played, as well as when and how the rules would apply."

GUIDING LIGHTS: *(clockwise from left)* Delia's parents, who instilled in Delia and her brothers the passion to reach for the stars, cut their wedding cake on December 7, 1956. • Walter Viader was a telecommunications advisor with the military in his early years. • Delia's mother, Delia, who grew up in a military family, felt right at home on her many travels with Walter.

A GENERATION BEFORE: *(clockwise from top left)* Delia's mother poses with her sister, Martha Alicia Esviza, who would later become Delia's godmother. • Delia's father, Walter, a diplomatic attaché, was noted for his calm demeanor. • The elder Delia *(left)*, Walter *(center)*, and Martha Esviza *(right)* stand arm-in-arm. • A young Walter enjoys a day on the beach with his siblings.

Despite being busy with their occupations, Delia's parents were always passionate about broadening their children's horizons. As soon as Delia could read, Walter pointed her in the direction of his personal library. She would read recommended books and then father and daughter would discuss them afterward. *What did the author mean? What had she learned?*

This was the era of John F. Kennedy's address to Congress pronouncing the goal of putting a man on the moon before the end of the century. Delia vividly recalls watching with her family and the world, on July 20, 1969, as Neil Armstrong stepped for the first time on the moon and proclaimed, "That's one small step for man, one giant leap for mankind." There was something in Armstrong's later comment about his landing on the moon that profoundly resonated with Delia: "Mystery creates wonder, and wonder is the basis of man's desire to understand."

EARLY DAYS: *(above and right)* Delia as a newborn lying safely in her mother's arms. • The cosmopolitan Viaders traveled extensively; here, they are pictured on a trip to Italy when Delia was just a few years old.

"We were all taught from an early age to reach for the stars," Delia says; it was one of the lessons she was most appreciative of receiving from her parents. She recalls also hearing Dr. Martin Luther King Jr.'s famous 1963 exhortation, "I have a dream." Such were the influences that Delia was exposed to as a child, the ways of looking at life that her parents taught her to emulate. "There wasn't anything that you couldn't achieve if you really wanted it. There wasn't any barrier that would prevent you from reaching your dream if you worked hard enough and poured all your passion into it."

For young Delia, when her parents were traveling, the older generation was an important part of her life. And while Delia's maternal grandparents did not get to meet any of the grandchildren, her paternal grandparents were close while she was growing up. "I remember sitting on my paternal grandfather's lap," she says. "And we would go through this adorable bonding game, every time he would ask me, '*WHO* are you?' I would proudly answer, '*Catalan.*' '*WHAT* are you?' and I would scream, '*Free*,' in the loudest voice my little lungs could muster.

"I learned that before I was two years old, before I even knew my whole name. It was so very important to him. It was in my grandfather's blood, imprinted in his mind. It wasn't a political affiliation; it was a way of *being* for him."

At the dawn of the twentieth century, Delia's paternal grandfather—tall, blue-eyed Joan Pedro Rafael Viader—was part of the landed aristocracy in Barcelona, Spain, a position his family had held

---

Father and daughter share in both looks and spirit.

"BICHITO" AND HER BROTHERS: *(clockwise from above)* Delia, Christian, and Walter Jr., sit with Annette, one of their childhood nannies. • Walter Jr. and Delia receive their First Communion. • Delia with her youngest brother, Christian, who, along with Walter Jr., nicknamed Delia *bicho*, which means "bug."

for generations. However, when Generalissimo Francisco Franco's agrarian reforms led to the seizure of Joan Pedro's lands in return for only pennies on the dollar, depriving him of his primary source of income, Joan Pedro was confronted with a difficult decision. So, he flipped a coin: heads, they would go to North America; tails, South America. The coin toss came up tails, so that's where he would start life anew.

Once in Buenos Aires with his family—including three-year-old Walter, an older sister, and later, a younger brother—Joan struck up a partnership with future shipping magnate Aristotle Onassis. They would grow tobacco in the northern provinces of Argentina and then produce and export exquisite hand-rolled cigars that would compete head-to-head with the legendary Cohibas of Cuba.

"My grandfather had no college education," Delia says. "When you had

land and you lived off that land, you didn't really need to go to a university. But he was extremely bright business-wise." Soon he had many more successes, exporting goods wisely. Over time, he managed to acquire many parcels of land.

With her parents so often posted in faraway lands for long periods, Delia spent a lot of time with her paternal grandparents, and Joan's entrepreneurial mind found in his granddaughter a kindred soul, even at a young age. "He was a free spirit, with the kindest, clear-water blue eyes," says Delia. She would always remember the lessons he taught her.

ANCESTRY: *(clockwise from top left)* Juan Norberto Esviza, Delia's maternal grandfather. • Delia Esther Suarez de Esviza, who, along with her husband, never got to meet any of their grandchildren. • Joan Pedro Rafael Viader, when he lived as one of the landed aristocracy in pre-Franco Spain. • Joan, Delia's paternal grandfather, who reestablished the Viader family in Buenos Aires. • Emilia Marrugat de Viader, Delia's paternal grandmother.

An Inquisition

WHEN DELIA WAS FIVE years old, she was placed in Paulina von Mallinckrodt Schule, a school for girls where she would spend the next twelve years—and where the operative word was *discipline*. "German nuns had no idea what *psychology* meant, let alone how to use it," Delia remembers.

There, she and the other students followed a traditional German Gymnasium program, which meant a thoroughly classical education, including learning ancient Greek and Latin for Mass. During these formative years, Delia was the equivalent of a straight-A student, with a good head for math, history, and science.

But she was also very inquisitive, delighted to discover beneath a complex surface an elegantly simple concept to explain why things are the way they are. "My mind was always racing ahead looking for connections. I had a reputation among the nuns for being troublesome, due to my never-ending questioning. I guess I had no fear. I always asked, politely, 'And why is it this way, and not that way?' I wasn't being rude; I just had questions, because the nuns only provided beginnings, which led to my many more questions about everything. I had a very deep need to know more. I particularly drove my theology teacher (an Armenian Catholic priest) crazy. I could make him go completely red-faced with frustration at times."

Consequently, Delia was often given time-outs, sent to a room and put "in isolation." There and elsewhere, she could read to her heart's content. Reading became her biggest pastime; there was no television at school. "My only way outside of those four walls was a book," she says, "and reading still is my favorite pastime." Her favorite authors? Albert Camus, who gave her hope, and Martin Heidegger, whom she found rewarding because his books were challenging and reading in his original German language was so hard to interpret.

RIGOROUS EDUCATION: *(right)* Delia, in the traditional dress for her First Communion. • *(following spread)* This 1975 class photo shows the all-girl student body of Paulina von Mallinckrodt Schule, where Delia, who was cultivating her questioning nature, spent twelve years learning under the German Gymnasium program.

GROWING UP VIADER: *(above and right)* Delia dressed up for
Carnival in 1966. • Delia, age 6, and Wally Jr., age 4, play by a
teepee in the backyard of their weekend house.

On holidays or stays at home, she would return to her grandparents' house. "I got very close to them," she says, "not only because they took care of me when I was little, but throughout."

Sadly, her grandma had had a series of debilitating strokes, after which Delia was taught by her grandfather how to take care of her, how to help feed her, to soften and brighten up her day. When her grandmother died, Delia was about twelve years old, and her grandfather, after more than fifty years of marriage, died of a broken heart shortly thereafter. These were hard blows for a young girl growing up on her own; but the spirit, support, and wisdom that her grandparents handed down would stay with Delia long after they passed on.

Landed at Fifteen

"I THINK I'VE ALWAYS had an entrepreneurial spirit," Delia says. "A different way of seeing things even at an early age . . . I was always dreaming ahead and entertaining so many possible outcomes."

This entrepreneurial spirit was on display when, instead of a *quinceañera*—the traditional Latin American celebration (typically, a Mass followed by a big party) to mark a girl's fifteenth birthday and to symbolize her transition from childhood to adulthood—Delia wanted property. She asked her father how much the whole festive affair would cost him, so Walter gave her a number and joked, "Are you worried that I won't do something good enough?"

"No," his daughter replied. "I just wanted to know how much I have to 'invest' because I don't want a *quinceañera*. I'd rather have something else."

Perhaps bemused, her father asked, "Well, what do you want?"

"I've heard that there is a new real estate development in the south, by the beach in Pinamar. Instead of giving me a party that is going to come and go, I want to get a piece of dune by the beach with a view of the ocean in my name."

"But you can't have it in your name. You're a minor."

That didn't matter to Delia. A piece of paper from her father that said it was hers, even if the legal deed was in his name, would be good enough. So, Walter went to have a look at the new development and ended up buying two pieces of land. He would build on one, and years later his daughter would build on the other.

In addition to becoming a land-owning teenager by the time she finished boarding school, Delia could converse fluently in six languages: English ("because mom would make us"), German ("because, of course, I went to a German school"), Italian, French, Spanish, and Portuguese, but the last only when she felt like it. "It's more Brazilian Portuguese," she says. "When I go to Lisbon or Porto, they hear my accent. It's like somebody from New Orleans or Mississippi talking to you. It's the same English, but it sounds kind of funny."

Her learning was impressive, her self-discipline well developed, and her education—thanks to many parallel university-level courses in high school—advanced, all of which would allow her to thrive in her next stop: Paris, France.

Walter Viader and sixteen-year-old Delia, pictured here at the weekend house with one of the family dogs, shared an entrepreneurial spirit. When Delia turned fifteen the year before, she told her father she didn't want the traditional *quinceañera*—instead, she wanted to make a deal to buy property. Years down the road, they would both have houses on the beachfront land he bought for her.

THE SEVENTIES: *(left and above)* When Walter became a diplomatic attaché, he and his wife, Delia, traveled all over the world. • Delia, age 15, lounges with a friend.

SIBLING REVELRY: *(clockwise from above)* Delia's brothers, Walter Jr. *(left)* and Chris *(right)*, pictured here in the '70s in London, were and remain very close. • Delia and Walter Jr. at a market in 1981. Years later, "Wally" would be a great help to Delia when she moved to the United States with her first three kids all under the age of six. • Delia holds a puppy at the beach house in Pinamar in the '70s. • Chris and Delia ride around on mopeds in 1981.

HOME SWEET HOMES: *(left and above)* Delia standing in front her house in La Lucila, Province of Buenos Aires. • Delia's father built his house on one of two plots of land he purchased in Pinamar at the behest of his fifteen-year-old daughter. The Viader family also kept other residences in the area, including houses in Hurlingham outside the main city and a ranch south of the nearby city of Coronel Suárez.

In Defense of Meaning

DELIA'S NATURAL TENDENCY to question everything, along with a feeling that maybe she should follow in her father's footsteps, led her to Paris and the Sorbonne. In 1976, she set up a new life in her parents' apartment in the 1st arrondissement. Once again in the heart of an international metropolis, she felt just as at home in Paris as she did in Buenos Aires. "When people asked me, 'But… you're Argentinean, right?' I replied, 'I was just born there.' I could have been born anywhere in Europe, in any other city; it would have been the same."

But despite her cosmopolitan lifestyle, diplomacy wasn't for her. "I realized early on that as much as I admired my dad, I didn't have the personality," she says. "You can read in my face when I'm bored. You can read in my face when I don't agree with you, and I'm very vocal about it."

Instead, Delia gravitated toward a field in which her pursuit of both abstract and objective answers fit in naturally: philosophy, with a concentration in logic. "I marveled at the dialectical way of thinking, the mathematical exactitude logic provided. I have always been fascinated by ideas and wanted to connect the dots in history, in science, in philosophy. I wanted 'truth,' and I was going to get to the bottom of it. Philosophy fit the bill, because you're always questioning everything to the irreducible first principle. I still keep at it, searching, reading, and debating with friends in academia. In that sense, I'm a true philosopher."

This lifelong pursuit of truth faced one of its earliest trials in the form of famed thinker and writer Jean-Paul Sartre. "There was always a select group that would be allowed to take a course with him, which wasn't really a course," she says. "It was just sitting in a café and debating. I always had opinions, but he considered me 'the little one with green eyes who pretends to do philosophy.' He thought I wasn't 'authentic' enough and that I wasn't 'aware' enough. He would practically pick on me because of that. I was seventeen years old."

On occasion, she could almost cry out of frustration when she couldn't rebut Sartre's insistence that we—our existence—is of no consequence; her being in the world thoroughly futile. Sartre would tell her, "Don't you realize that there is nothing after this? Do you realize that you are today the *decrepit cadaver* that

Delia, pictured here right before she went to the Sorbonne, in Paris, where she received her PhD in philosophy, with a concentration in logic.

you will become? It's only a question of time; there is no meaning for you, no essential reason of your being here." But Delia could not accept that defeatist lack of hope.

It's very possible this conflict of viewpoints was simply a result of two wildly different life experiences: Sartre was someone who had lived through two horrible, bloody World Wars, whereas Delia was an educated young woman coming of age in the mid-1970s. "We'd always have very lively conversations," she says. "I thought it was natural for everybody to be in this natural quest for meaning, or at least trying to lead a meaningful life. It's not a question of ego, it's not a question of leaving a trace, but a question of believing our lives have purpose."

Another experience that separated the purposeful student from her existential teacher was the advent of parenthood. When Delia was fifteen, she met an Argentinean of Dutch roots at the beach in Pinamar, and the two became inseparable. They eventually married, and their first child, Paul, was born with Down syndrome in November of 1978. Delia and her husband, still students without full-time jobs, were under pressure to give up their baby and put him in an institution that would know how to better care for him. "But I remember answering almost in anger to the 'suggestion' that I wasn't going to refuse a child just because he was not the flavor I wanted," she says. "It was difficult for the whole family to accept that Paul came perhaps with not all the possibilities. But I was going to do everything in my power to make it right. Whatever potential he had, he was going to reach it. Of that I had no doubt.

"And when Paul was born, that definitely made me realize that there *is* a purpose in life," she emphasizes. "The moment you become a parent, you realize that it's not only a tremendous responsibility when you take up the task of caring for this very tiny person, who is totally vulnerable, but you also realize that there is a bigger purpose, and you want to change the entire world, make it better for your child. That's what every parent wants. In China or in Timbuktu, you want to provide something better for your child."

Delia plays with her sons Paul (*right*) and Alan (*left*) in front of her future beach house in Pinamar in 1982. After receiving her doctorate in Paris, Delia had to decide where she and her young children were going to live, eventually choosing the United States, based at least in part on the opportunities and resources available for Paul, who was born with Down syndrome.

STABLE TRIADS: *(clockwise from top left)* Delia and her mom with Janet, Paul, and Alan in the United States in the late 1980s. • The three kids smile in front of the Christmas tree. • Walter Sr., Delia, and Walter Jr. take the kids out for the day. • The new trio of siblings in the Viader family—Alan, Paul, and Janet—are still very close, much like Delia and her brothers. The trend of Viader trios would later continue when Delia's brother Christian and his wife, Silvia, welcomed triplets.

Delia cared for Paul while completing her work at the Sorbonne. When her thesis—on the concept of freedom and its evolution through the writings of the great philosophers, from Thomas Aquinas through the Existentialists—was accepted, she received her doctorate of philosophy. So, what next?

"My very first priority was to take care of my kids," she says. "And I knew that there were not many opportunities to provide for Paul back in Argentina." Delia had a degree and, by this point, three little children. Like her grandfather, she had to decide where to go. Argentina was out. The countries that offered the most possibilities for Paul and his condition were Switzerland, Germany, and the United States. "The United States was my third choice," she says.

But her younger brother, Walter Jr., was pursuing his own studies at the Massachusetts Institute of Technology (MIT) as an engineer in electronics. Delia saw this as an opportunity and asked her Dad to pay for three more years of education plus room and board while at MIT.

"I said, 'Dad, can you do two for one?'" She was accepted to the Executive Financial program at MIT's Sloan School of Management. She had to convince a few people, as well as her brother Wally, to share responsibilities with the children's care, but she persevered.

"Just tell me, 'No, it can't be done,' and I will say, 'Just watch me.'"

The kids go skiing in Tahoe with their Uncle Chris, 1987.

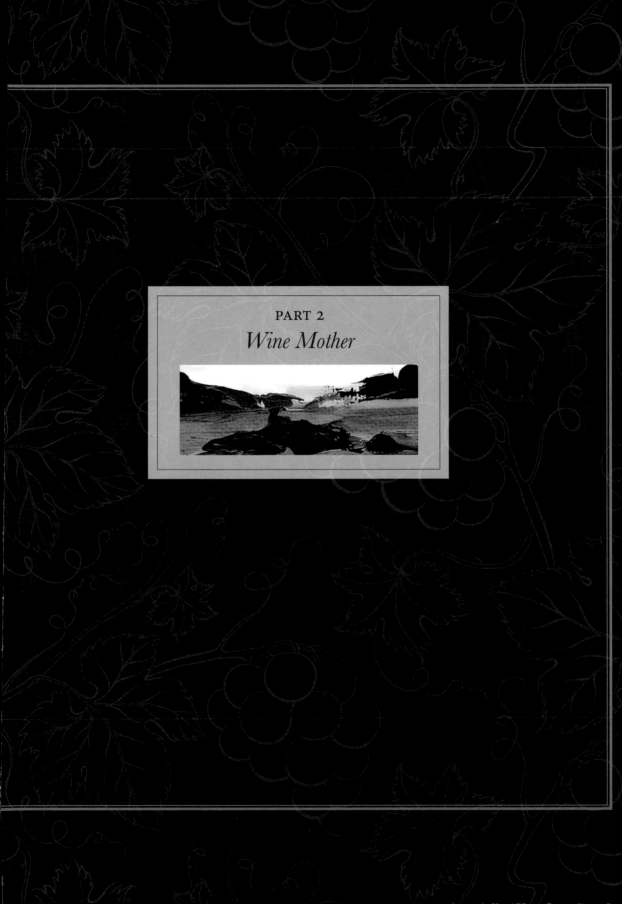

PART 2
Wine Mother

A Home on
Howell Mountain

"THERE WERE A LOT of personal trials and tribulations during this time," Delia says of the years following the Sorbonne. "I was everywhere and no-where. Luckily my brother Wally came to live with us, and he was great with the children."

By the early 1980s, she and Walter Jr. had decided to move to California, "My first love was Napa Valley—not necessarily wine," Delia says. "I saw a lot of opportunity, but I couldn't find a job I wanted, even though I had good business skills."

There were other issues as well: Delia needed to make her divorce legal (which was luckily easier to do in the United States than in Catholic Argentina), as well as change her student visa to an H-1B visa, available to those immigrating with advanced degrees. To do so meant translating each course of the whole curriculum she'd taken at the Sorbonne into English and obtaining equivalency at the University of California–Berkeley, a process that took years. It also meant passing all the normal "elective" courses in American civics and history of the United States. "I really enjoyed that part," she says, "because I always loved history."

Thankfully, by 1985, things started to coalesce. A friend of a friend, Ric Forman, was showing a piece of property for sale as a possible housing development on Howell Mountain, near Angwin in Napa Valley. Walter Sr. was approached about forming a partnership to develop the land, plant a vineyard, and create a winery. He was going to be their financial backer, but his daughter had a more familial alternative.

"I said, 'Dad, if you put up all the money, I think I can make this work

---

HOWELL MOUNTAIN: *(left)* An overhead shot of the plot of land on Howell Mountain where Delia would build her vineyard shows the large rock fixtures, which proved to be so challenging to work with they had to be dynamited. • *(following pages)* Paul, Alan, Janet, the family dog, and Delia pose on the porch of their new home on Howell Mountain.

When Delia, pictured here in 1984, moved to Napa Valley, her first love was the land, not necessarily the wine industry. She ended up creating a winery, but it was born from opportunity and necessity— the desire to build a home for her family.

by myself,'" Delia recalls, attracted to the challenge. "I imagined this place as becoming an ideal refuge up in the mountains. I saw the potential of a home for my family, working in such a way that my children could be part of it and with me, all the time, in this idyllic setting, in this quiet, very small town. That's when I decided, *I can do this*. When my father remarked for the first time 'After all the money I poured into your education, all you want is to become a farmer?' I assured him, 'Yes, Dad.'"

Hard as it may be to imagine now, vineyard land in Napa Valley was not expensive back then. The glamour of today wasn't there, but the infinite complexity of wine and the unique microclimate and terroir of this special property became Delia's all-consuming passion.

"I didn't know exactly how, but it was a perfect opportunity to come in. The barriers to entry were low in an industry that was awakening from the dormancy of Prohibition at the time."

Despite five intervening decades, the wine industry in the United States was still reeling from the scourge of Prohibition, which went into effect in 1920 and lasted a full thirteen years. That time saw so many wineries close down; most vineyards were abandoned or replanted with lower-quality varieties for use in home winemaking. After repeal in 1933, pre-Prohibition wineries like Krug (founded in 1861), Schramsberg (1862), Beringer (1876), Inglenook (1879), Larkmead (1895), and Beaulieu Vineyard (BV, 1900), joined by Martini in 1933 and others, led the way forward. Wine still wasn't widely consumed or very well known in the United States, but all that would start to change, particularly after Robert Mondavi opened his winery in 1966.

When Delia arrived, there was a feeling of a new beginning in the Napa Valley, even if it was mostly aspirational. "However serious I was, my father wasn't going to lend me any money unless I presented a feasible business plan. That was critical to my pursuit. No banks were lending money to start a vineyard, and at the time, my thinking was that you had to have a vineyard in order to start a wine brand."

So she drew up her new business plan to make it all possible. The plan was outlined on the basis that her father would invest more and more in the project over the course of the first seven years. In many ways, Walter Sr. was taking a big chance with the deal. But despite the risks—and no doubt confident that his daughter could make the project a success—he agreed to fully finance Delia's new endeavor.

"The next thing I needed to do was negotiate the terms of the property purchase," Delia says—which proved to be no easy task. The problem was that the owners of the land, Alice and Chester Cooley, didn't necessarily want to sell their land to someone living outside of the community. Napa Valley, especially St. Helena, was a small and tight-knit community then—everyone knew one another. And the Cooleys wanted the sale to be settled through a series of payments, which they would rely on to sustain them in their retirement years. Could they trust this young outsider? After all, Delia was still attending UC Berkeley, commuting from the East Bay every day while the children attended

school in San Ramon. Once again, in many ways it would be taking a chance for the Cooley's to make the deal with Delia.

But, as she has done so effectively so many times throughout her career that's followed, Delia listened. She recognized the instinctive concerns the Cooley's might have, and her training kicked in. A promissory note, recorded with the deed of trust, would guarantee the sellers a comfortable and secure stream of money for retirement. More importantly, when they found out that Delia wanted to provide a home and an income for her young children, they committed to the deal. Clearly, they saw that buying the land wasn't *just* a business deal for Delia—it was about creating a home, and connecting with the area. "That is what they wanted all along," she says. "Suddenly becoming a wine grower looked possible. I'd created my own job."

CHALLENGING TERRAIN: *(left and above)* Many thought building a viable vineyard on the rocky slopes, with a mere eight inches of top soil, would be impossible to pull off. The machinery couldn't handle it, they said, and the plants wouldn't take. Delia did it anyway. • Delia's innovation of planting tightly-spaced rows and a nonterraced layout for maximum sun exposure has now become a widely adopted vineyard practice on these kinds of rocky slopes.

Although she wasn't consciously aware of it at the time, Delia Viader was returning to the lifestyle her grandfather had when growing up near Barcelona. "In a way, I grew up without setting roots anywhere," she says. "I had been going around like the stone that gathers no moss. So, to me, it was also a discovery of a place I could call home, somewhere where I could plant roots and raise my children. I had fallen in love with the beauty of the Napa Valley. It felt right. It was a very important moment in my life and those of my children."

And Delia was going to be putting down roots quite literally.

Planting the vineyard was clearly going to be the biggest challenge. At first glance, her place on Howell Mountain was nothing but mottled rock and a mess of poison oak. Making the land hospitable to her new vines would take some serious work. And even after the plants were in the ground, it would be another four years before the first commercial grape crop could be harvested, and a further three years to produce a satisfactory red wine. All told, it would be a minimum of seven years before she saw much more than a penny in return.

"You're in the wrong business if you're looking for a quick fix," Delia says. "Grape growing for fine wine requires a long-term view. In jest, I call it 'sophisticated farming.'

"It was a discovery of a place I could call home."

Surely, it is farming at its core, but there is a heightened attention to detail and an unparalleled level of sophistication in a vineyard, with a focus on the correlation between rootstock and grape variety, and the interaction of the vine with the soil, that produces that special grape."

Delia also had to form her winemaking team, and in typical fashion, she wanted nothing but the best. "It was learn-on-the-go, right from the beginning," she says. "I believed that my site's terroir could produce a first-class vineyard and a special wine that could rival the best wines of Europe. It's not that I love Europe because it's Europe. It's that in winemaking, they have at least a few hundred years' experience, and I wanted to avail myself of their expertise."

HARD WORK: *(clockwise from top)* When Delia purchased her little corner of Howell Mountain, the plot was little more than rocks and poison oak. An immense amount of work went into making the ground hospitable for her new vines. • Sheep lounge and munch on grass among the vineyard stakes. • Vineyard workers break up the rocky soil with post-hole diggers, readying the ground for planting.

At the time, most vines in the Napa Valley were planted on flat valley floors or on hillsides on contoured terraces. Delia's team of experts proposed something altogether different, specifically designed for her site—a layout that took into consideration everything from the composition of her soils to the angle of the sun to the diurnal-nocturnal temperature differentials at different altitudes and the direction of the afternoon breeze. The ultimate goal was to produce wine grapes of the highest quality in the most natural and pesticide-free way possible.

Every aspect of vineyard blocking and row construction was also scrutinized, covering direction, density, and even the layout of dirt avenues within the vineyard. Each grape varietal was planted on a top-to-bottom continuum using

---

A STAR IS BORN: *(above and right)* To gain a year, the vines are grown in a nursery in cardboard containers. • Delia's Cabernet vines take hold. It can take seven or eight years from the time of planting until selling the first bottle: three to four years from planting to commercial harvest, then two years for fermentation and barrel aging, and then another two years of maturing in the bottle.

an east-west row direction without any terraces, allowing the vines to absorb every minute of sunshine.

In sum, every detail of the vineyard layout was carefully engineered and executed to address specific elements of the site's geography. All these elements would contribute to long-term sustainability and to the production of world-class VIADER wines.

This kind of vineyard design was not conventional, at least not at that time. Prohibition had put a clamp on vintners' pioneering spirits and their desire to innovate. Those classically American traits were cast aside as the vintners struggled to survive.

But Delia was an innovator by nature. "My approach was not the norm," she says. "A wine wasn't thought out in those terms from the ground up. Being a mom first, thinking of setting up a home for my family, kept me motivated, and because I grew up with a different background, I was doing this from a completely new perspective."

In fact, the land itself demanded a new perspective; for example, terracing wasn't really an option on this hillside. "With our kind of soils and configuration, to terrace and compensate for the steep slope would leave too much terrain totally unprotected from erosion. We specifically designed the vineyard to optimize the site with high-density planting of 2,200 plants per acre on a 5-x-4 configuration—five feet between rows and four feet between vines—all nonterraced and noncultivated, with rotating cover crops in between rows. This added massive root coverage and promoted soil retention compared to the existing naturally growing grasses and sparse brush vegetation." This layout also allowed Delia to extract the highest-quality juice from each berry, at a low output per vine but with an overall financially feasible yield of two and a half to three tons per acre depending on the weather conditions of the particular growing season.

The concept was simple: smaller vines planted at a high density per acre would compete on the ground for the few available nutrients. This has several advantages, according to Delia. "The type of grafting rootstock chosen had relatively high vigor that would send very deep tap roots into the soil to protect the vine from the long summer months without rain during the growing season in California. The vines would be kept smaller by the very low fertility of the soil combined with less irrigation (deficit irrigation) at the correct time during the vegetative cycle of the vine. Literally our little 'bonsai' vines cling to life on the hill."

The vines are kept valiantly erect with the hanging fruit zone much closer to the ground, as in Burgundy, France. Because of this, the grapes have to be hand harvested, a laborious process that has to be done on your knees. But low-hanging grape clusters also means that the fruit benefits from a band of heat radiating from the volcanic rock in the soil right after sunset, every single day of the growing season. The cumulative effect is that VIADER's grapes mature perfectly sometimes seven to fourteen days ahead of neighboring properties and well before the late-autumn rains.

Delia interviewed several possible experts for the Herculean job of preparing the soil for her site-specific vineyard layout. "Some of them looked at me like I had three heads," she says. "They quipped that it is practically impossible to maneuver heavy machinery on such a steep slope. At the time, there were no small tractors of ultracompact girth designed to work in so tight a spacing between rows—only five feet apart—let alone with enough grip to not roll when working on a steep angle. The norm then was spacing rows twelve feet apart because a tractor needed that much space to get through. My goal was to produce the highest-quality grapes as a start of a higher-caliber wine. And a wine . . . is made in the vineyard."

Years later, tightly spaced, high-density planting would become the norm for high-quality vineyards, as growers and vintners sought greater intensity and concentration of flavors within each berry. And the agricultural industry would respond in kind with advanced technology, including "crawler" type mini-tractors that could work on steep hillsides, pulling the equivalent of several hard-working horses.

Innovation returned to the wine industry, offering many labor-saving ad-vantages. Delia explains, "What at one point kept me in super good shape, having to walk the vineyards daily, my son Alan can now tap on his iPhone and gather information from our many different sensor points on the ground and within the vine at various parts, useful information on every parameter imaginable. Yet, I still like to go down a vineyard row and visually check that my 'babies' are

all right; my dog never far, as the prevailing rocks make for an excellent habitat for rattlesnakes, as well as raccoons, coyotes, foxes, squirrels, and the occasional black bear, all of which take their share of grapes near harvest time."

In Europe, Delia had grown accustomed to seeing very tiny vines producing excellent fruit while barely clinging to life. In such places as Germany, Switzerland, Spain, and Burgundy, each of the vines would be individually tended to, and the vineyards worked completely by hand, with the occasional help of heavy-duty horses.

After an extensive search, Delia finally found the vineyard manager to execute her plan. David Abreu, a third-generation St. Helena rancher who would later become the most sought-after hillside vineyard manager in the Napa Valley— and eventually be recognized as the most successful, meticulous, and influential vineyard manager of all time—accepted the challenge. David was joined by viticulture consultants Danny Schuster from New Zealand, an expert in hillside organic farming, and Richard Nagaoka, the "Grape Doctor." Also included were consulting winemaker Tony Soter, who was winemaker at nearby Spottswoode in St. Helena, and who would later found his own namesake Pinot Noir vineyard and winery in Oregon; and Delia herself. Together, they comprised the VIADER vineyard and wine team that would make Delia's dream a reality.

Some might have stopped there, but Delia also requested the professional opinion of longtime friends and experts Michel Rolland, who was the winemaker and estate manager at his family's Château Le Bon Pasteur, and Jean-Claude Berrouet, the longtime winemaker at Château Pétrus, both from Bordeaux. "At that time, Michel Rolland wasn't even thinking about becoming the most highly paid and sought-after consulting winemaker in the world," she says. "But I always felt very much at home with the French language and French traditions."

Delia's connection—and Napa Valley's connection—with France was so close and strong that she and her friends formed a close-knit group and jokingly call themselves "the French Mafia." Delia describes the alliance: "We were all

---

FRUITS OF HER LABOR: *(top to bottom)* Delia was closely involved with the production of her vineyard. • Years later, her careful oversight was evident as her legacy vines took hold. • *(following spread)* Delia walks through her young vineyard in 1987 with consulting winemaker Tony Soter, checking on her rootstock. The land on which the vineyard is situated drops four hundred feet in elevation between one vineyard block and the next.

away from home and missed our family traditions in this newly adopted home of ours, so we became close friends. Our children were of similar ages and growing up under the influence of both cultures, so we said, 'Might as well band together and hang out together.' And we often did. I have fond memories of sharing a *Réveillon de Nöel* (a family gathering on Christmas Eve) every year, with a big long table for the adults, filled with lots of traditional dishes and, of course, numerous bottles of French, American, Chilean, and other wines . . . and then, another long table for the children where French and English could be heard intermittently." It became a well-known secret in the valley that every intern who couldn't go home for the holidays was invited to this *Réveillon* with the Viader family on Christmas Eve.

Delia had found her team of experts, and they not only helped her build VIADER wine from the ground up, but they also helped her create the home on Howell Mountain she so wanted for her family. A good sign that she was on the right track was when they were cleaning brush off the hillside and found the telltale signs of perfectly aligned tomato stakes, evenly spaced, which meant that part of her hillside already had been a nonterraced vineyard planted decades before, perhaps during the nineteenth century—and perhaps by earlier Frenchmen Brun and Chaix. Delia knows with certainty that her property was part of the lands of the Rossini family of Swiss-Italian origin. They also planted vineyards in the area of Howell Mountain where Francis and Françoise DeWavrin-Woltner had a Chardonnay vineyard, which was later changed to Cabernet Sauvignon by Pat Stotesbery of Ladera, above Delia's property.

> *In Europe, Delia had grown accustomed to seeing tiny vines producing excellent fruit.*

THE A-TEAM: *(clockwise from top left)* Consulting winemaker Tony Soter was also winemaker with Spottswoode in St. Helena at the time Delia recruited him for her team of experts. • David Abreu crouches next to one of the VIADER vines. David was the only vineyard manager who accepted the challenge of creating a world-class vineyard on the unforgiving slopes of Howell Mountain. • Delia and a few of her team of experts discuss the vineyard: *(left to right)* David Abreu; Delia; Jean-Claude Berrouet, winemaker at Château Pétrus; Daniel Baron, winemaker at Silver Oak; and Tony Soter.

Dynamite Vineyard

TO PREPARE THE SOIL, make it suitable to receive the plants, and to soften up the enormous quantities of volcanic tuff, basalt, and rhyolite rock in the future vineyard, Delia had to resort to "low to the ground" explosives in some sections that were too difficult to work with a normal hydraulic augur hammer attached to a D10 tractor. "You need to crack the bedrock in order to give the vines a possibility to explore those cracks with their roots. So, this is literally a *dynamited* vineyard." Delia again recruited specialists, this time from Portland, Oregon, and Washington, engineers who knew how to apply low doses of dynamite for maximum effect.

Later, the laborious job of planting the vines would involve the use of jack-hammers to create some sort of "natural" rock pot, where, in Delia's words, "very daring vines would produce the tiniest of berries with the most incredible black and plummy flavored juice."

NURTURE VS. NATURE: *(left and above)* Alex sits on top of a forklift, an appropriately kid-sized variety of the heavy-duty machinery put to use for the construction and maintenance of the VIADER vineyard. • The maneuvering of big machines and vehicles on the side of Howell Mountain was one of the hardest parts of constructing the vineyard, as powerful hydraulic augers mounted on tractors had to be used to break up the rocky ground. When the augers didn't work, low-level explosives were used instead.

Support System

DURING THESE YEARS of planning, recruiting, and explosions, Delia continued to make personal connections. "There's more in Napa Valley than just the fantastic soil," she says. "It's the fantastic people we have in the valley who impart a sense of community, a unique type of camaraderie akin almost to an extended family." She particularly appreciated the sharing of information and the encouragement that Robert (Bob) Mondavi offered to anyone in any position and of any origin within the wine industry. Many of the families whose names today grace the labels of Napa Valley's best bottles cite Bob Mondavi as their inspiration.

Bob's wife, Margrit Biever Mondavi, became one of Delia's dearest friends. Margrit's philosophical approach to life and enduring optimism was something Delia admired. "Her love and support for the creative and culinary arts was a

"There's more in Napa Valley than just the fantastic soil."

testament to her open-minded nature," Delia says. "Plus, we could always communicate in any language, especially French. Swiss-born Margrit had no difficulty switching from German to French or Italian within the same conversation." Delia and Margrit delighted in speaking multiple languages, eliciting comments of admiration from Bob every time.

Because Delia was planting the vineyards first and building the winery later, she needed to find a winery where she could have her first wines made under a "custom crush" agreement. She rented space at Rombauer Vineyards, a newly built winery, which, from 1987 to 1998, served as her home base.

At Rombauer, Delia shared space with the John Daniel Society, whose wine project was called Dominus. There she met Christian Moueix, the owner of Château Pétrus, a partner in that venture. "There were many happy connections with friends of friends of friends," Delia says. "It was mostly high-end wine growers who shared common European traditions and who appreciated great wine and food. For me, being here alone with my kids without any other family support, it was like having the support of a huge extended family. Every single one of them helped me, with their advice and inspiration, to realize my dream."

Delia stands with her dear friend Margrit Mondavi while vacationing in Morocco. Margrit was part of a support system of friends and colleagues that welcomed Delia to Napa Valley and helped her truly see it as her new home. Margrit was born in Switzerland, and she and Delia would often converse in a variety of languages, including French, German, and Italian.

Plato & Patience

IT WAS TIME FOR DELIA to select the right rootstock and the appropriate grape varieties to plant in her vineyard. "I knew very little about growing grapes, but I knew what I liked in a fine wine," Delia says. "What I liked was wine of a certain caliber. I had been raised with wine served at meals every day since an early age. At one family dinner, when I was barely a teenager, I tasted a wine . . . smelled a wine from Bordeaux, and I will never forget its seductive aromatics. The complexity of the bouquet and everlasting flavors piqued my interest like nothing else before. That memory still lingers today."

To bolster her knowledge, Delia started taking viticulture courses at the University of California–Davis. "At some point, even Christian (Moueix) joined, too, because we both wanted to learn more. UC Davis was addressing industry-relevant topics in a series of RAVE lectures (Recent Advances in Viticulture and Enology)," she says. "I would heed what the best consultants would advise, but I also wanted to learn myself and understand the details. I always return to academia. I have this unsurpassed thirst for learning and desire to hear from different voices, evaluate different perspectives, until I figure out which is the best path that's going to take me to where I want to go."

Delia approached her choice of rootstock using the Socratic method. In Napa Valley, most winemakers order grapes of French origin, imported into the United States from ENTAV (Etablissement National Technique pour l'Amélioration de la Viticulture or National Educational Association for Viticultural Improvement) by licensed nurseries that sell the certified genetic material. After long and deliberate consideration, Delia decided on Cabernet Sauvignon, Cabernet Franc, and Petit Verdot grapes, and a moderate to vigorous rootstock, 110 R, which is resistant to phylloxera. "And that's what saved me," she says.

A marker in the VIADER vineyard indicates the type of grape that is planted in that section. Delia's vineyards include an array of varietals, including Cabernet Sauvignon, Cabernet Franc, Petit Verdot, Malbec, and Syrah.

THE MAKING OF A VINEYARD: *(clockwise from top left)* Workers put in the end posts that will support the training wires and hold irrigation lines. • Holes needed to be drilled into the rock in order to plant the vines. • Delia specifically designed the vineyard to optimize the site with high-density planting. • Sheep wander through the vineyard's rows, mowing the grass. • VIADER's huge water storage tanks are constructed by hand.

Some growers at that time were still working with rootstocks that were nonresistant to phylloxera, the same nasty root louse that all but destroyed European and American vineyards in the nineteenth century by attacking *Vitis vinifera* vines. Ultimately, the vineyards were saved by grafting *Vitis vinifera* grape vines onto naturally resistant native American rootstock. But that came only after a major devastation.

The resurgence of phylloxera in the mid-1980s in Napa Valley caused a great deal of damage, too, decimating 70 percent of the planted acreage. The affected vines were planted on AXR#1 rootstock, a cross between *Vitis vinifera* and *Vitis rupestris*. Though nonresistant, AXR was very easy to plant and provided a good "take," which would more or less guarantee abundant yields before the disease took hold, if ever. Delia avoided AXR altogether.

"I considered that plan to be plain folly," she says. "From day one my focus had been on producing wine of the utmost quality. Making wine in abundance from diseased grapevines was utterly ridiculous to me. I decided to wait until a rootstock that was resistant was available and not take a chance." The delay, though well advised, was more than a full planting season.

Delia's parents retired from public service in 1989 and were spending half the year in the

"I have this unsurpassed thirst for learning."

Catalan area of Sitges, Spain, and the other half in Buenos Aires. They would often visit Delia and their grandchildren on their way back and forth, for several weeks at a time. They saw all of their daughter's work, as Delia explains, "proceeding in an 'ant-like' progression, completing piece by piece a gigantic puzzle that existed only in my mind." That "puzzle" was starting to take shape, the result of Delia's vision and tireless efforts.

Delia stands with her mom and dad in front of her eponymous vineyard, which was painstakingly constructed and cultivated. Their support—both emotionally and financially—was a big factor in enabling Delia to realize her dreams.

BEYOND THE VINEYARDS: *(clockwise from left)* A rock path winds up the slope of Howell Mountain, near the tasting room. • Delia walks her dogs on the grounds outside the tasting room. • Looking down across the Syrah vineyard that went in some years after the first VIADER vineyard. • The seasonal beauty of Napa Valley is what inspired Delia to create a life here. • One of the many fountains on the VIADER grounds, which were positioned to optimize propitious feng shui principles.

Founding a Home

"FIRST THE VINEYARD and then the house—contrary to everybody's idea that I should have the winery first," Delia says. "Because we couldn't live in the winery." That is how the VIADER wine estate developed.

When the resistant rootstock arrived in 1986, Delia planted her first twelve acres of closely spaced rows of Cabernet Sauvignon, Cabernet Franc, and Petit Verdot grapes, using budwood from neighboring vineyards that Delia believed were producing wines of exceptional quality. These twelve acres were subsequently expanded to twenty-eight acres, with the addition of grape varieties like Malbec (from Argentina, which Delia's son Alan had come to appreciate during his harvest internship there) and Syrah (two different clonal selections, one hailing from Barossa Valley, Australia—known there as Shiraz—and the other from France's Rhone area).

Each clone had its own unique rhythm: Its vegetative cycle was unique, but all the other variables—soil, rootstock, sun exposure, and cultivation practices—were the same. One clone of Shiraz would always ripen before the other. Alan took this further in 2002, in the cellar, using fermentations of various lengths to build texture and further highlight in each wine its unique flavor profile.

Delia believes that the most important aspect of the vines' growth, besides adequate sun and rain, is the composition of the soil. "The survival of the species depends on passing along the seeds inside the fruit. The vines are unique organisms that reflect and translate their microcosmos through their fruit, taking very little from the soil. Vines can live for a hundred years, and wine . . . wine '*is bottled poetry*,'" Delia explains, referring to a quote from Robert Louis Stevenson's *The Silverado Squatters*, a travel memoir of the author's honeymoon in the Napa Valley, published in 1883.

Mountainside vines grown in volcanic soils often produce the most distinctive wines. Before Prohibition, Howell Mountain had been renowned for its many bountiful vineyards, and its exceptional wines were reputed to have a distinctive flavor and superior quality.

Delia, pictured here in her new house in 1991, which was built to the contours of the mountain, had her home completed before she started on the winery so that her family would have a place to live. In the intervening years, the *Ficus benjamina* planted in a planter in the middle of the living room grew from its original five-gallon pot size to the ceiling height of twenty-two feet.

The winter months of 1989 were devoted to the building of the family home, which would have a breathtaking view of the valley and her hillside vineyard. Years before, on the beach plot that her father had purchased for her, Delia had built a house around a tree in order to have a small interior garden. She did the same on Howell Mountain, working with architect Richard MacRae from Sebastopol so that the roots—again, literally planting roots—of the *Ficus benjamina* she chose would reach directly into the earth beneath the home's foundation.

The final part of her construction plan was the winery, with its associated network of tunneled caves that would pull together the entire estate. Each undertaking—house, tunnels, winery—was a massive project taken in baby steps.

THE MAKING OF A HOME: *(clockwise from above)* Janet, Delia, Paul, and Alan enjoy family time together. • Scaffolding is set up for work being done on the Viader home in 1991. • Delia had the family home built just uphill from her vineyard on Howell Mountain, and it enjoys an expansive view of the valley below. • *(following spread)* A view of Delia's estate shows just how close to the vines the house actually is.

The Terroir

"THERE IS SOMETHING truly special in Howell Mountain's reddish soil," says Delia. "This is a fantastic terroir, and by *terroir*, I mean the combination of many elements: soil, rocks, the angle at which the sun hits that soil, and the human environment; the hands of the men and women cultivating it."

Located 1,300 feet above the Napa Valley floor on the Vaca Mountain range east of St. Helena, VIADER sits on a toe slope of Howell Mountain over the rich remnants of a former volcano. Its ancient rocks and sandy loam red soils—Forward-Aiken soil series—are mineral rich, and particularly iron rich, which gives it the distinctive reddish coloring.

During the growing season, which is characterized by Napa Valley's classic Mediterranean climate of cool, wet winters and hot, dry summers, the volcanic rock absorbs and retains the day's intense heat, releasing it after sunset to maintain a gentle, even ripening of the grapes. The result is perfect physiological maturity of the berries. With so little topsoil, the vines are favorably stressed and compelled to commit every drop of their resources to the production of berries, not leaves. By forcing the vine to concentrate its efforts on the fruit and flavor development inside the berries, which carry the seeds that guarantee the survival of the species, a wine's unique flavor is literally "made" in the vineyard itself.

"With the vines planted closer to the ground, creating that gentle ripening effect, and countless hours dedicated to ensuring that every detail of the site was enhanced and optimized to provide that extra 'élan' in the fruit zone, our first harvest was in our sights," recounts Delia. "It was so close, I could taste it."

HOWELL MOUNTAIN HARVEST: *(clockwise from top)* Vineyard workers pick grapes by the light of their headlamps, as night falls over Howell Mountain (photo by Luisa Bonachea). • Workers gather grapes for the crush, and Janet makes sure no leaves get mixed in with the grapes (photo by Luisa Bonachea). • Kodi, VIADER's quality volunteer tester, on location. • *(following spread, left to right)* Winemaker Alan Viader holds Cabernet Franc grapes after fermentation. • More in keeping with the planting techniques of European wineries, VIADER did not use terraces for their grapes, instead planting their vines in east-west rows, up and down the steep hill.

Memory of a Season after Rilke

And you wait, await the one thing,
that will infinitely increase your life;
the gigantic, the stupendous,
the awakening of stones and sun and light;
the depths and distances turned 'round towards you.

The volumes of crimson and gold
glimpsed dimly in the cellar aisles,
make you think of vineyards travelled through,
of weather, of the labors
of vines found and lost.

And then all at once you know that was it
You rise, and there stands before you
the fear and prayer and shape
of a finished year.

WINTER WONDERLAND: *(clockwise from top left)* The vines on Howell Mountain stand bare and blanketed in snow. Weather like this is fine while the vines are in their winter dormant stage, but vineyard managers must be careful to prevent frost damage if temperatures drop below freezing in the early spring when new shoots are forming. • The dramatic, sloping roof of the VIADER winery is covered in a rare occurrence of winter snow. • The door to the cellars, pictured here in 2000, defends against the encroaching cold, keeping the maturing wine inside at a safe and stable temperature.

First Vintage

IN 1989, DELIA AND HER TEAM produced the very first vintage of VIADER, her signature wine. The wine is a blend of Cabernet Sauvignon with a high proportion of Cabernet Franc, affectionately called "Liquid Cashmere." "It had that European elegance reminiscent of Bordeaux in aromatic texture and density," she says, "which somehow captivated wine connoisseurs at first taste." She decided to put her family name on the label and asked local artist Chuck House to present various options that reflected the wine's place of origin. Also, as a creative marketing tactic, she decided to print the winery name and phone number on every cork, thereby creating a sort of "portable" business card for customers enjoying her wine. "Everybody in my team was shocked by that idea . . . 'They will know where to find you,' " she says. "My response was, 'So? If I'm going to make the best wine this site can produce, I'm going to stamp my name on it. And I *want* people to know where to find my wine.'"

VIADER's first bottled vintage produced a mere 1,200 cases of wine.

Although Delia had produced small batches of wine in 1987 and 1988 at Rombauer's winery (where VIADER was made for the first eleven years), she wasn't pleased with the results and did not bottle them. "I sold it all in bulk," she says. "I needed to come out with something very special to show the result of all this work, a first wine that would be good enough so I could start repaying my father. Until that point, everything had been a big black hole money-wise, as it always is during the first seven or eight years in the wine business. You have to wait four years at least to have a decent crop and three more years to produce a red wine, then you wait and hope and pray and hope again that customers and wine critics will like it."

VIADER's first bottled vintage produced a mere 1,200 cases of wine, which Delia offered first in Europe—taking advantage of her ability to communicate fluently in several languages—where it was very well received. It was a start.

"I never imagined not succeeding, but it wasn't very clear right then and there how I could succeed. Europe to me seemed so much more manageable

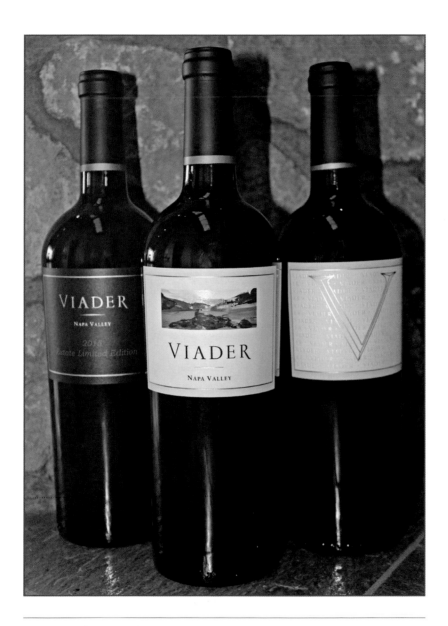

After waiting four years to have a decent crop and another few years to produce a red, the first VIADER vintage came in 1989 and produced a mere 1,200 cases of wine. Local artist Chuck House designed the label, per Delia's instructions, and each bottle is hand-labeled.

THE WINEMAKER AND HIS TEAM: *(clockwise from top left)* Alan draws a sample of wine for blending. The process is subtle and takes years of practice, which Alan has been dedicated to since he was young. • Notepad and pen are always close at hand for tasting notes while Alan does his blending. • Workers carry bins of freshly picked grapes. • The dedicated vineyard team is hard at work during the busy and laborious harvest season. • Alan shares a moment with Delia, who has mentored him closely as he trained with Michel Rolland for five vintages, to become VIADER's winemaker.

as a first market. You don't need to convince people in Europe, where wine is an integral part of a meal. Most of them grow up with wine as part of their everyday lives."

As a single mother and a foreigner, a veritable fish out of water, Delia faced challenges adapting to life in America. Some aspects of the culture were initially unknown to her. "One time I remember casually asking in conversation who Elvis Presley was, only to be looked at as if I had just landed from Mars," she says. "My accent was also an item of constant conversation; to me, it made me self-conscious, yet everyone kept saying it sounded delightful."

In the summer of 1990, with her kids out of school in the East Bay, Delia moved the family into their new house in Deer Park—a family that grew by one with the birth of Alexandre, her youngest son, in December of 1993.

NATURAL PROGRESSION: *(above and right)* Delia smiles with her certificate on her Naturalization Day, June 6, 2006. • Alex, the newest member of the Viader family born in December of 1993, stands in the family vineyards.

During those globe-trotting years when Delia was building and positioning her brand all over Europe, Asia, Latin America, and the United States, she had excellent helpers in Monica Gonzalez Bautista and later Blanca Avina, who could take care of the children while their winemaker mom toured the world presenting and selling her wine.

"I grew up in the vineyard," son Alan says. "My backyard was the hills where I could run freely." Alan fondly remembers those early childhood years in Napa Valley. "My mother would bring me along during her vineyard walks, tasting and checking the grapes' maturity levels. Wine growing became part of my life. Each summer vacation was spent working in the vineyards. Sometimes I would have to

EXPANSION: *(above and right)* Blanca and Monica attend Alan and Mariela's wedding in July 2006. Mariela is head chef at Viader. • Viader's award-winning red blend reflects Delia's wine-making philosophy of creating subtle characteristics by coaxing the variety to show at its best.

take time off of school for harvest and to help in the cellar, racking wines, cleaning barrels, and dragging hoses. Once home after school, I would be put on the schedule to help with pump overs. Every facet of my life revolved around wine."

Delia educated all of her children about wine. She would have them taste wines and ask what they thought about the specific "taste" and "feel" of different varieties, then discuss the soils where those grapes had been grown, and so on. "Mom entertained friends at home quite a bit when we were growing up," her daughter Janet recalls. "So, the dinner table was always full of wines from all over the world."

"My mother talked to me about the history of the property and the unique characteristics of its soil," Alan adds. "She also spoke about her winemaking philosophy, her desire to create subtle elegance by coaxing the variety to show at

its best, to produce these very fine, subtle characteristics in the wines through their gentle interaction with what nature provided. She spoke of terroir and the influence of the seasonal vagaries of weather—all present in the finished product."

Delia's children were all given the opportunity to work in the cellar from an early age, "waking up" the yeast in a bucket and even shoveling out must (the skin and seeds of the grapes) from the fermentation tanks. "I always enjoyed the energy and the excitement of harvest time," says Alan.

And Alex recalls, "I was eager to help any way I could, even though I wasn't always strong enough to keep up with my big brother."

FAMILY PORTRAITS: *(clockwise from above)* Delia and the kids visit her parents in Sitges, Spain, for Walter Viader's eightieth birthday in 2001—*(left to right)* Janet, Delia the younger, Alex, Walter, Delia the elder, and Alan. • Paul, Delia's eldest, in 2017, at the age of thirty-nine. • Alan tries out the new grape press in 2006. • The newest member of the family, Alexandre, was born in 1993, expanding the trio into a quartet. • Janet Viader on a trip to Kathmandu, the capital of Nepal, when she was seventeen years old.

Delia presents VIADER's entries at the Bad Ragaz Wine Festival in Switzerland. Her passion for her wine and her winery are evident in her tireless efforts to promote her brand—throughout the 1990s, Delia would travel every other week to more than thirty countries, opening accounts in every market by herself.

The European Connection

WHEN SHE WASN'T in Boston or Napa, Delia was abroad, maintaining those one-on-one relationships necessary to make certain her wines received their due. This included participating in myriad events of major importance around the globe, such as judging Rieslings in Germany, engaging in competitions with top masters in Switzerland, and so on. A typical European jaunt would last nine days and include seven countries: a show in Cologne or Munich or Frankfurt, the opening of a "big-deal" eatery in Berlin, or perhaps a tasting of the best "New World wine," which she would present (in French, of course) in comparison to an "Old World wine" such as Château Cheval Blanc, presented by Pierre Lurton at an exclusive establishment in Luxembourg, or at Le George V restaurant in Paris, or at Alain Ducasse's restaurant in Monaco.

"Once I was seated with the general manager of a famous First Growth from Bordeaux," Delia says. "We were in Switzerland at a long, well-orchestrated affair where all the wines were presented in a blind tasting, through several flights, and we both thought, *Oh, I think I've tasted my wine. I think I can vote and vouch for this one. It's really very, very good.* And most probably we were voting for each other's wine, which ended up being super interesting and the subject of many jokes between us."

Throughout her travels and global work, *discipline* was always Delia's sustaining byword, along with her natural enthusiasm. "When you present what you're so proud of, the passion shines through," she says. "If you're not passionate, you won't survive in the wine business. I do enjoy it. I definitely enjoy the creative aspect and the sharing of it with friends."

Every other week throughout the 1990s and 2000s, Delia was on the go, traveling to more than thirty countries and opening accounts in every market by herself. Her ability to speak several languages became a huge asset. "I was the face of the wine and the winery," she says. "It was truly a one-woman show."

Because Delia prized European winemaking culture, she concentrated her energies there. "My marketing focus was different from the norm," she says. "I wanted to present my wines in the bigger pond of the world rather than what

THE
WINE
BAR
GINZA

WIFE
WOMEN
WINE

I considered the smaller pond of the United States. I'd always considered Europe—and Bordeaux, in particular—as having the greatest masters in the art of winemaking. It keeps you honest and humble to work side by side with brand owners who have over two hundred years of history over you."

Delia wanted to compete with the real players, to vie with them at the top. But just as important, she wanted to set herself apart—stand beside, not imitate, those storied wines of the Old World. "I want to produce wines that have a sense of place and that provide the best expression of their varietal characteristics," Delia says. "I want to succeed with wine in the same way that an artist or craftsperson works with his or her medium. In my wines, I like to compose the aromatic profile first, texture and density second, and nuances that leave a lingering, pleasant memory in the palate last. When tasted side by side, each grape variety has a distinct personality that emerges within the vineyard itself, plus the seasonal capturing of the weather characteristics by the vines growing and interpreting a specific site. All of that correlation becomes what could be described as a 'family trait.' I want my family trait to be wines that are fragrant with fine and silky, evolving tannins, never overwhelming—a wine that does not 'shout' at your palate, but instead whispers seductively, a wine that keeps you interested after the first sip."

INTERNATIONAL PRESENCE: *(clockwise from top left)* Delia with Daniel Gantenbein in Switzerland. • Delia in Tokyo working to put VIADER on another international wine list. • This certificate is signed by attendees of Churchill's Graham's A.G.M. Lunch in Porto, Portugal. The British club only allows women to attend its events on very special occasions. In this case, Delia was invited by the Symington family, who can trace their lineage in Port back to the seventeenth century. • In Porto, Portugal, Delia and friends crush grapes with their feet in a lagar, which is a type of open-top fermenting tank. This is part of the traditional process for making port.

The 1990s were indeed a golden era for Napa Valley. "All of a sudden people were starting to pay attention to Napa Valley," Delia says. "They actually were able to pinpoint where we were located. We started to have some notoriety. It wasn't that people didn't appreciate our wines, it's just that they didn't expect such quality wines to come from the United States, because so very few small producers in America would think of exporting their wines then." But Delia was ahead of the curve on that front, and her instincts would soon pay off.

Whether in Napa Valley or abroad, Delia never considered being a woman to be a handicap. "It didn't enter my mind," she says. "In the States, it probably was an Old Boy's Club; for somebody born in the United States, it probably is. For me, coming with no preconceived ideas, it wasn't. You see, I wasn't out to shatter the glass ceiling, because I never thought there was one. My education at home had been completely gender neutral."

Delia wanted to set herself apart—stand beside, not imitate, those storied wines of the Old Word.

Of course, Delia did encounter some chauvinism, but it was directed at her wines, not her. "There was a Frenchman who absolutely did not want to taste my wines because they were not French," she says. "While we were talking and talking, however, he said, 'Well, your French is pretty good.' He says, 'Maybe.' And I said, 'You can taste it and spit it out,' so he finally tasted my wine. He ended up liking it very much, but so astonished and embarrassed was he, that he didn't know how to tell me that. He really had never liked a wine that wasn't French. Finally, he figured that because I wasn't American, he could be allowed to like my wine."

INDUSTRY ASSOCIATES: *(top and bottom)* Delia sits with two of her closest friends, giants of the Napa wine industry, Peter and Bob Mondavi. • Delia visits with Mrs. Lee *(left)*, of Nara (the South Korean importer for VIADER and Shafer wines), and Barbara Shafer, while on a trip to Seoul, South Korea, in 2002.

Château
Mouton Rothschild
33250 Pauillac
France

-

Tél.: 05 56 73 21 21
Fax: 05 56 73 21 20
Tél International :
33 5 56 73 21 21
Fax International :
33 5 56 73 21 20

TELECOPIE / TELEFAX

DATE   June 15, 2004 _____ HEURE _____ _____

DE / FROM Baroness Philippine de ROTHSCHILD _____

A / TO   _____

ATTN   Mrs Delia VIADER _____

N° FAX   00 1 707 963 38 17 _____ _____

NOMBRE DE PAGES / NUMBER OF PAGES _____1_____ _____

(Cette couverture incluse / This page included)

Dear Delia,

Many, many thanks for your charming letter accompanying the wonderful present of your wine which you sent me at Mouton.

I am very touched by this generous gesture, and I shall taste the 2000 and the 2001 as soon as I get back to Mouton in two weeks.

I believe we shall meet in Italy at the Antinori's PFV trip.

So, looking forward to see you,

Yours fondly,

Philippine

NOTABLE CORRESPONDENCE: *(above and right)* Baroness Philippine de Rothschild, who was the owner of one of France's finest wine houses, Château Mouton Rothschild, thanked Delia for sending VIADER wine. Her father, Baron Philippe de Rothschild, started Opus One Winery in Napa Valley with Robert Mondavi. • Robert and Margrit Mondavi, who were some of Delia's dearest friends, welcomed her with open arms when she first arrived in Napa.

June 24, 2004

Delia Viader
Viader Vineyards & Winery
PO Box 280
Deer Park, CA 94576

Dear Delia:

You certainly know how to get to a man's heart. That Ferragamo tie is a beauty — the dog reminds me of Luce many times over. Thank you, Delia, you are indeed very experienced and knowledgeable.

God bless you.

As always,

Bob

Robert Mondavi

RM:mja

ROBE

A

P.O. Box 106   Oakville, California 94

June 24, 2004

Delia Viader
P.O box 280
Deer Park, CA 94576

Dear Delia:

It has been too long since we last saw you but we hope you are having a happy summer somewhere beautiful. Thank you very much for the great tie you chose for Bob's birthday.... so many little Luces and my absolutely favorite color. He will wear it often because he too loves it and because I insist. Please call sometimes so we can get together.

With much love,

Margrit and Bob

Margrit and Bob

cc: RGM

MBM: cd

ROBERT MONDAVI WINERY
POST OFFICE BOX 106 OAKVILLE, CA 94562
TEL. 707.226.1395

Tunneling Through a Mountain

THE EARLY YEARS continued to be hectic. Delia was on the road, still building her business, and still learning. "I had a lot of things happening at the same time," she says. "After the house was finished, next came the winery—and I'd always envisioned that the house and the winery would be connected via tunnels. Caves were something that was just beginning to become popular but that made a lot of sense in the mountain."

Delia met with Alf Burtleson, a general engineering contractor specializing in the construction of wine caves, and said, "I would like the first tunnel to go from this end to the other side. And once you reach the other side, I would like you to put a small window in that exit door, because I want to be able to see the light at the end of the tunnel."

The "light" became a running source of laughter between them, because hers would be the only cave of about forty in Napa Valley, at the time, with a window exit at the end.

The first tunnel would be 250 linear feet long. Eventually, six more tunnels were added in stages, starting each time from the outside and intersecting with previous tunnels below. The tunnels had to work from both an engineering and a winemaking perspective, given that the entire winery is "housed" underground, preserving untouched the beautiful mountain manzanita and chaparral vegetation on top. While the excavation and construction continued, the VIADER winery had to remain operational throughout. Fortunately, emerging technology was a big help, enabling Delia and her crews to pinpoint cave connections, even thirty-five feet underground.

Delia contracted Alf Burtleson to construct a series of tunnels and caves, which were just starting to become popular in Napa Valley, to connect the house and the winery. The window in the door, which was a feature unique to VIADER's tunnel system, was requested by Delia because she wanted to be able to "see the light at the end of the tunnel."

BURIED TREASURE: *(clockwise from top left)* Tunneling through the solid basalt rock required a very large drill, which on some days would only progress a foot. • Casks filled with VIADER's wine, aging until just the right moment, line the sides of the tunnels under Howell Mountain. • Members of the family delve into the darkness of the unfinished cave. • The cave nears completion.

ARCHITECTURAL SPLENDOR: *(clockwise from top left)* Delia's winemaking knowledge and skills are perfectly suited to the relatively small scale of the winery. • The winery, with its ornate arched front entry door, dramatic slanted roofs, and stone siding covering the entire exterior, takes its cues from the hilly terrain, which provides gravity feed to several types of fermenting vessels. • The fermenting tanks fit through the doors with mere inches to spare.

Double Success

DURING THE SUMMER OF 2000, Delia received excellent news: the 1997 VIADER, her signature blend of Cabernet Sauvignon and Cabernet Franc, was going to be part of the Top 100 best wines of the year, as chosen by *Wine Spectator* magazine. The December 31, 2000, issue posted the actual rankings, and 1997 VIADER was #2 of the Top 100, described as "beautifully proportioned, rich and complex, ripe . . . currant, black cherry, mocha, toasty oak and spice . . . silky on a long, elegant finish."

To arrive at its final appraisal, the judges at *Wine Spectator* had tasted over the previous year more than 11,000 newly released wines in blind tastings, of which more than 1,550 were rated 90 points or better. These superior wines then became candidates for the Top 100. Final rankings had been determined by four criteria: quality (score), value (price), availability (as measured by production), and an X-factor called "excitement."

"Our 1997 vintage was the best on record," Delia says. "It was one of those gifts of God that only happens once in a lifetime. We had a fantastic crop and we had it in abundance. We made the wine, selecting the best as usual with no compromises. It's a nice feeling when you feel, *I think I'm there*; when you start to see that success is within reach, because it's not just you, but people of influence see it and appreciate it, too."

At the time, Alan was going to school in Sonoma County, working various jobs to pay his student bills, and he ended up hearing the news indirectly. "One of the guests at a local golf club where I was working recognized my last name and started a conversation," Alan says. "He was very pleased to meet me and couldn't say enough good things about the VIADER wines in his cellar. I kept having more and more encounters like that."

The new millennium went off with a bang for VIADER winery. The December 31, 2000, issue of *Wine Spectator* magazine ranked the 1997 VIADER as the #2 wine in the world in its prestigious Top 100 list. That vintage was quickly followed by the 1998 VIADER, which came in at #3 on the 2001 list. Delia had a lot to dance about at a holiday event held in the cellar.

Janet, then enrolled at the University of California–Berkeley, was very proud to see her mother's picture published in *Wine Spectator*. "Although I was just entering college and technically not of legal age to taste wine," says Janet, "I was already well-educated about it and developing my wine palate. Like my mother, I would host secret blind tastings with friends, even before the reviews came out." You do not gain knowledge and appreciation for wine unless it is presented to you as an ordinary part of a meal. Delia's children learned like she did, at an early age, to have an appreciation for fine wine at the table.

Janet was born in 1982, a spectacular vintage in Bordeaux. Delia is well aware of this happy coincidence. "Since her late teens, we have been celebrating Janet's birthday with superb Bordeaux, something that becomes challenging to improve upon and very costly as she grows older."

The following year, more ecstatic reviews: Delia's 1998 VIADER red blend was ranked #3 in *Wine Spectator*'s Top 100 Wines of 2001. "In only 10 vintages, VIADER has established itself as one of California's top reds," wrote the *Spectator*. "Even more remarkable, it achieved a classic rating (95) in the extremely difficult 1998 vintage."

1997 VIADER was #2 of the Wine Spectator's Top 100.

"VIADER came in number three, number two being Cheval Blanc," Delia says. "That was a huge deal for me, because it was with a 1998 vintage, a very challenging year to grow grapes in California, but a very good vintage in Saint-Émilion, Bordeaux."

Not only had competition been fierce, but El Niño—a periodic weather phenomenon that brings much more rain than normal to the California region—had made achieving a good harvest that year much more difficult.

"Getting national recognition twice was an even sweeter victory," says Delia.

Janet remembers more photos of her mother in *Wine Spectator* and other wine industry publications. She assisted in compiling press kits to spread the word. "That's how I got started in the family business," says Janet. "Even during school breaks, it was always 'all hands on deck' and contributing to the best of your ability."

This article, published in 2015 in *Robb Report*, a luxury-lifestyle magazine, is one of many that Delia and her family have been featured in over the years.

Philosopher's Stones

MOTHER AND SON OVERCOME ALL OBSTACLES AT VIADER.

WHAT HAPPENS WHEN an irresistible force meets an immovable object? In Delia Viader's case, a vineyard is planted. The native of Argentina discovered California's Napa Valley in the early 1980s and decided to put down roots—literally. Most vineyards at that time were situated in the richer alluvial soils of the valley floor, but Delia—who had at the time no training in oenology, though she holds a Ph.D. in philosophy from the Sorbonne in Paris—chose a site on the slopes of Howell Mountain. The steep parcel offered ideal sun exposure; its soil composition, however, was almost entirely rock. When Caterpillar D9s failed to remove these immovable obstacles, Delia turned to an even more irresistible force: explosives.

"We kept breaking equipment that was never supposed to break," recalls Delia's son, Alan, who now serves as director of operations for Viader but was, at the time of these excavations, just a boy. "So there was dynamite involved, and even then, some of the rocks were so large that the only way to move them was to push them downhill. There are still sections of the property that we can't plant, because they're 100 percent rock."

These stones became Alan's nemeses. "I had the very unglamorous job of moving rocks out of the vineyard growth," he laughs. Yet his mother—who undertook intensive oenological studies at the University of California, Davis—rewarded him and his siblings for their contributions by tutoring them in the appreciation of fine wine,

including the best of Bordeaux and Burgundy. "She would always break them down," he says, "and tell us what we should be tasting and smelling."

The release of Viader's inaugural vintage, 1989—a classic, balanced blend of Cabernet Sauvignon and Cabernet Franc—and its successors soon elevated Viader to the top tier of California producers, and Delia, Alan, and his sister Janet continue to build on their reputation for terroir-driven beauty.

Delia's style from the start emphasized elegance, finesse, and aromatics, rather than ripeness and power; and Alan, on taking up daily responsibility for the winery, pursues that same goal, while adding his own touches. "One thing I've increased is the stirring of the lees, which adds more

mouthfeel, complexity, and roundness," he says. "She jokes that I like a little more toast."

The most recent releases of the flagship wine, the Viader 2011 and 2012 Liquid Cashmere Proprietary Red Blend ($150), exhibit Delia's preference for aromatics and the greater weight resulting from Alan's barrel regimen. A cooler vintage, 2011 presents aromas of strawberry, Bing cherry, and rhubarb—and, on the palate, flavors of red currant, cinnamon, allspice, and mint. In contrast, 2012 reflects a warm, even growing season: deep, ineluctable essences of rose petal, raspberry, black cherry, marzipan, and vanilla.

"Everything was ideal," notes Alan of the 2012 vintage, though he concedes that his old adversaries, the rocks, proved his allies in 2011. "It was cold, wet, and gloomy, but," he adds cheerily, "because of my rock, the rain drained right through."

—BRETT ANDERSON

Viader, 707.963.3816, *viader.com*

CATHY O'HAGAIN

THE TOP 100 WINES OF 2000

Wine Spectator [...] released wines i[...] year 2000, of which more than 1,550 rated 90 points or better. These were the initial candida[...] Our final rankings were determined by evaluating each wine on four criteria: quality (as repre[...] reflected by price); availability (as measured by production or, in the case of international wines[...] an X-factor we call excitement.

Red wines rose to the top of the heap, comprising more than three-quarters of our Top 100[...] success of three important wine regions—extraordinary vintages in 1997 for California Cabern[...] outstanding vintage in 1998 for France's Southern Rhône Valley. For complete tasting n[...] www.winespectator.com. Tasting coordinator James Molesworth contributed to Top 100 profiles[...]

We hope you enjoy *Wine Spectator*'s 2000 Top 100, with its mix of blue chips and values, collectib[...]

Wine Spectator
www.winespectator.com

THE TOP 100
The Most Exciting Wines of 2000

PLUS:
OUR EDITORS SELECT
THE "WINE OF THE YEAR"

Holiday Champagnes
And Sparkling Wines

Piedmont's Great
'96s and '97s

More Than 400
New Wines Reviewed

DEC. 31, 2000–JAN. 15, 2001
$3.95 US $4.95 CAN

Delia Viader

2

VIADER
Napa Valley 1997 • 97 / $60
CALIFORNIA

Delia Viader's red debuted with the 1989 vintage and first graced our Top 100 in 1997, with its 1994 vintage. Winemaker Tony Soter, who has since retired from consulting, notched this Cabernet Sauvignon-Cabernet Franc blend a little higher with this vintage. It's Viader's best effort to date, and well-priced, too. 4,800 cases made.

Thomas Leonardini

3

WHITEHALL LANE
Cabernet Sauvignon Napa Valley Reserve 1997 • 97 / $60
CALIFORNIA

Whitehall Lane wines just keep getting better. The 1997 Reserve is made from grapes grown on the estate's Leonardini vineyard and grapes purchased from Morisoli vineyard. The '97 Napa Cabernet bottling was our No. 72 wine last year, while the '95 Reserve made it all the way to No. 5 on the 1998 Top 100. Kudos to Thomas Leonardini and his winemaking staff. 2,850 cases made.

Lucien Michel

4

LE VIEUX DONJON
Châteauneuf-du-Pape 1998 • 97 / $25
FRANCE

Lucien Michel makes his Châteauneuf-du-Pape red using traditional methods. Two-thirds of the 29.5 acres of vines producing fruit for this wine are between 80 and 100 years old. Michel believes the '98 could match the quality of the 1990, which he describes as "our mythical wine." 4,165 cases made.

Wine Spectator magazine editors have been reviewing the best wines in the world since 1988, and VIADER wines have met their exacting standards. Listing VIADER #2 in the December 2000 edition was a breakthrough for the company, and it was the culmination of all of Delia's hard work over the previous two decades.

Pierre Lurton

Delia Viader

Ettore Falvo

2

CHÂTEAU CHEVAL-BLANC

St.-Emilion 1998 • 98 / $190

BORDEAUX

One of the more successful
Bordeaux appellations in 1998,
St.-Emilion boasts dozens of
excellent wines. Cheval-Blanc
represents the pinnacle. A wine
of great breeding and distinc-
tion, the 1998 is director and
winemaker Pierre Lurton's best
ever and one of the greatest
Cheval-Blancs ever produced,
challenging, and perhaps in time
eclipsing, the classic wines from
1982, 1985 and 1986. 8,330
cases made.

3

VIADER

Napa Valley 1998 • 95 / $65

CALIFORNIA

In only 10 vintages, Viader has
established itself as one of
California's top reds. Even more
remarkable, it achieved a classic
rating in the extremely difficult
'98 vintage. Tony Soter, who
retired from consulting in 1999,
worked with winemaker Delia
Viader on this blend of
Cabernet Sauvignon and
Cabernet Franc. Viader farms 28
acres of vines on Howell Mountain. 3,500 cases made.

4

AVIGNONESI

Vino Nobile di Montepulciano
Grandi Annate Riserva 1997
• 96 / $40

TUSCANY

Ettore, Alberto and Leonardo
Falvo have owned this domaine
since 1974. The Grandi Annate
Riserva, which comes from single vineyards in the Le Capez-
zine and I Poggetti estates, has
only been made twice before, in
1990 and 1993. Both previous
vintages used the traditional
Vino Nobile grape varieties: Prugnolo Gentile (the local Sangiovese clone), Canaiolo Nero and
Mammolino. For the 1997, 85
percent Prugnolo Gentile is sup-
plemented by 15 percent
Cabernet Sauvignon. 2,600
cases made.

DEC. 31, 2001 - JAN. 15, 2002 • WINE SPECTATOR **45**

Just one year after breaking into their top ten, *Wine Spectator* ranked VIADER at #3 on their Top 100 for 2001,
firmly establishing the winery as truly world-class.

The Next Phase

FOR ALAN, THE SEA CHANGE in the VIADER reputation didn't really sink in until after college when he started working full-time helping to manage the vineyards in 2002. In the years leading up to this, Delia's second-eldest son had bolstered his wine education by spending harvest time at many important wine regions in Argentina, Italy, France, Spain, and Portugal. At UC Davis, he'd studied viticulture. "The phones in the office would not stop ringing," he says of their winery's rise. "The voicemail was constantly full from people trying to place orders. Faxed order forms filled the paper tray, and the fax machine constantly needed to be replenished with paper. It felt surreal."

"I knew how hard my mother had worked to get us to that point," Alan says. "I knew I had to keep up that quality in our vineyard production. I had to maintain that high-level quality in our grapes; I took that very seriously. We were slowly transforming from a small winery trying to make the best wines possible, into a world-renowned brand; and yet we had so much more work ahead of us."

It was now Alan's turn to travel. He attended dozens of tasting events around the world while his mom and little Alex were often in Italy, developing a new vineyard in Tuscany from scratch.

Alex, in fact, spent so much time in Italy that he was able to converse fluently in Italian and often would take loads of homework to complete on plane rides. At nine years old, he could navigate the city of Florence like a native, and he still has fond memories of the time spent there from 1999 through December 2007.

Accolades continued to pour in. VIADER '99 graced the cover of *Wine Spectator*. Reporter Jim Laube wrote, "Starts off warm and inviting, with fragrant cedar, cocoa and truffle aromas, then develops concentrated black fruit flavors in the mouth. This smooth, medium-weight wine picks up some hints of tobacco on the finish and closes with just enough powdery tannins to give it structure. Delicious." "VIADER would always capture attention in Europe as part of New World winemaking versus Old World winemaking," Delia says. "Our wine was paired several times with Cheval Blanc, for example, just because my wine has so much Cabernet Franc in it."

In 2002, Alan graduated college and started to work full-time at VIADER as a vineyard manager, allowing him to start putting into practice all the training he'd received through school and internships abroad in places like Argentina, France, Spain, and Portugal. His guiding principle ever since has been to maintain the same exceptional quality that made VIADER famous all over the world.

Bolgheri: In Search of the Tuscan Sun (1999–2007)

MEANWHILE, DELIA was moving forward on the international front with an altogether new project. She had spotted a twenty-acre piece of land in Bolgheri, Italy, the small, special, and emerging wine-growing region of Tuscany and the birthplace of the legendary "Super Tuscans."

Delia says, "I would work two vineyard developments, in two different continents, a plane ride of eleven hours and nine time zones apart, during the same harvest month of September for eight years nonstop. If the fire of October 12, 2005, at Mare Island in Vallejo had never happened, my son Alan would still be doing what he grew up doing, and I would be traveling from Italy to visit my grandchildren."

In 1974, Bolgheri had become internationally known following an event in which a six-year-old Sassicaia red wine from the region had triumphed over an assortment of Bordeaux top wines. Delia entertained the idea that, if her now-grown children would run their Napa Valley operation, the twenty-acre property in Bolgheri (and the house in San Vincenzo) could be her retirement place in Italy where "life seems easier, the pace is slower."

In Italy, she would grow Merlot, Cabernet Franc, and Petit Verdot, not just to buck the Sangiovese tradition but because the soil and the area's climate made it imperative. She could apply her grape-growing and winemaking knowledge based on fifteen years of experience in Napa Valley and then learn even more.

When an old house in nearby San Vincenzo, Comune di Livorno, with no street address but carrying the auspicious name of Il Masseto, came up for sale, she jumped at the opportunity.

Janet and Alex pose for a picture at the door of Il Masseto, the house in San Vincenzo, Italy, that Delia bought around the time she was establishing a new vineyard in the auspicious Bolgheri region of Italy. If all had gone according to plan, Delia would likely have retired to this second home in the Tuscan countryside.

Il Masseto was only five miles (eight kilometers) away from the piece of land she would later plant with Merlot. The property's owner would occasionally commute from Germany to enjoy the Tuscan sun, but only every so often, so the house had fallen into disrepair. Nevertheless, its location atop a gentle hill, surrounded by about twenty acres of *macchia*, or natural forest, provided a breathtaking panoramic view, checkered with vineyards and red-tiled houses, along with cypresses and sunflowers, all sharing the stunning backdrop of the Tyrrhenian Sea beyond the village of San Vincenzo below.

Buying Il Masseto, the house, made perfect sense. "It was a crumbling old house, which I set out to put a lot of TLC into, only a short distance away from the vineyard in Bolgheri. It had a beautiful forest surrounding the house, on top of a hill with a panoramic view of the sea where you could see the island of Elba and on the clearest of days, you could even see Corsica. For me, the only way I knew how to 'retire' was to keep doing what you love doing."

A NEW VENTURE: *(clockwise from top left)* More than fifteen years after starting her first winery, Delia, accompanied by Ludwig Martel (VIADER's Swiss importer), assesses the new development in Bolgheri, Italy. • Walter, Janet, Delia the elder, and Alex enjoy the Italian countryside. • Alex stands at the end of one of the rows in the family's Bolgheri vineyard, next door to Ornellaia.

PLANTING ROOTS IN ITALY: *(clockwise from top)* The beautiful region of Tuscany in Italy was where Delia had planned to establish a small vineyard and eventually retire. • Delia's new vines grow in the light-reddish soil of the Bolgheri wine region. • Delia crouches beside the thriving vines of her Bolgheri vineyard. • Il Masseto, the old house in San Vincenzo, which Delia picked out as her home in Italy, was perched atop a small hill, providing a view of the glorious countryside.

"My mom never stops," Alan says. "From the vineyard to the winery, she's always pushing me to think bigger and long-term to continue improving. But that's what happens in small family operations; you're all so busy working *in* the business all the time."

Delia's staunchest supporters continued to be her family—her father, Walter, and mother, Delia, who would come by and visit often in Italy. "I would send my mom the magazines in which I appeared on the cover," Delia says. "She would gleefully show it off to friends and say, 'Oh, that's my daughter.' But whenever Dad was asked, 'What does your daughter do in the States precisely?' he would always say, 'Oh, she's a farmer.'"

As her fame grew, Delia was asked even more often if it had been hard to succeed because of her gender. "Why would you want to give me that advantage, or discount our ability?" she replied once to a journalist who was doing a story on women winemakers in Napa Valley. "Maybe we succeed because we're good at what we do."

The earlier chauvinism toward her Howell Mountain vineyards, however, had more or less evaporated. "Many years ago, when I was showing my wines abroad, people would tease me about these being American-produced wines," Delia recalls. "Now they say, 'Oh yes, grown in the Napa Valley, of course.' We have learned and advanced so much in the last few decades. American winemakers used to always be going to France to learn. Nowadays, the trend has reversed, and French enology students dream of coming here. For each year's harvest, we have a full crew of students from all over the world who want to learn in the Napa Valley."

LIFE IN TUSCANY: *(clockwise from left)* Delia jumped at the chance to buy Il Masseto, the old Tuscan villa she hoped to one day retire to. • Delia and Marilisa Allegrini with Chef Fulvio Pierangelini, owner of 3 Michelin–star San Vincenzo restaurant, Gambero Rosso. • Alex and Alan (with Chef Pierangelini in the background) enjoy a meal at Gambero Rosso. • The Viader children—Paul, Alex, Alan, and Janet—sit for a portrait in the late 1990s. • Delia poses with her mom, Delia, and Aunt Martha in Bolgheri, Italy.

Warehouse Torched

DELIA AGES HER WINE in small French oak barrels from twenty-four to thirty months in the tunnels underneath the winery. When finally ready, the wine is bottled on site with a small machine that bottles about two hundred cases a day. These bottles are then labeled by hand, one by one, and then tissue wrapped and set in a wooden box. Palletized on-site, the wines destined for distribution or export are then transferred by truck to a wine-storage cooperative warehouse in American Canyon. Typically, Delia keeps a small portion of her prized bottles—library and large formats—in the tunnels beneath her winery in Deer Park.

In 2005, a contractor who had promised to finish lengthening one of the tunnels *before* harvest fell behind schedule. Harvesting, producing, storing, bottling, and hand-labeling wine requires ample space, and the construction delay cut into that. Consequently, Delia had to move 7,400 cases of her 2003 vintage to be hand-labeled at a different location.

She sent those wines to Wines Central, an immense warehouse—a seemingly impenetrable, temperature-controlled fortress, housed in a former submarine hangar from 1942—because of its location on Mare Island, Vallejo, only thirty-five miles south. The warehouse was a major storage center for wine producers, given that it could hold 1.2 million cases of wine and had thick concrete walls that acted as a natural insulator and bulwark against earthquakes.

"The cases were there simply because I was expanding one of the tunnels," Delia says, "and we couldn't find a clean, straight, comfortable place where we could hand-label. There, they had plenty of space and were relatively close by. The bottles would be hand-labeled, set in wooden boxes and palletized for distribution from that location."

Small lights softly illuminate the long, arched tunnels below the mountain where VIADER wines age in oak barrels. Unfortunately, in 2005, one of these tunnels was still unfinished, forcing the fateful off-site storage of over seven thousand cases of the 2003 vintage.

On Wednesday, October 12, 2005, Delia was invited to a celebratory dinner at Meadowood Resort. She was attending as a guest of Silicon Valley Bank, well recognized in the wine industry. "I was being invited to listen to their analyst's presentation," Delia says. "So, they wanted to include me at the dinner, and it was a five-minute drive from home."

Back home, Alan had been working in the vineyard—it was still harvest time—when his phone rang. "A friend of mine working in the fire department had heard news of a five-alarm fire at Wines Central," Alan says. "He knew we had wine in that warehouse, because his family also had wine there. I dropped everything and rushed out to the warehouse in Vallejo. As soon as I saw the huge plume of smoke across the sky, I called my mom."

It was just after 6 P.M., and Delia was about to walk into the Victorian manor where the restaurant was located, when her phone chimed. She couldn't understand Alan at first. His voice was trembling. Something about a "warehouse fire." "Burning." "Total Loss." A feeling of doom flooded her. She needed to go, but she couldn't just turn tail and skip the dinner.

"It was a five-alarm blaze, a huge fire—and that's when I started to run numbers in my head," she says. "I thought, *I have insurance, how many cases do I have there?* This was right before the wine would be released for distribution. One-third of it was already sold, the other third was committed . . ." Thinking fast, she realized there was a razor-thin silver lining: Her bankers were inside, waiting for her.

VIADER's wines have a distinct personality—a taste, a feel, a look—and each vintage is unique. Losing the 2003 vintage in the Wines Central storage facility fire in October 2005 was akin to losing irreplaceable artwork. Yes, Delia would rebuild, but that particular wine was gone forever.

"She was calm and collected," Alan says. "She told me everything was going to be okay. I know, she was already twenty steps ahead in her head."

"Right at that dinner, I'm talking to the president of the bank," Delia remembers, "and I said, 'I think that to make it to the end of the year I'm going to need a bridge loan of about $1 million.' As I proceeded to explain the reasons behind my request, they were like, 'Sure, we can talk about that tomorrow.' Nobody could believe what I was saying. The fire was not even in the news yet. The enormity of all this was already apparent to me, but not yet to them."

"It was devastating for me," Alan says. "Watching the fire blazing with dozens of fire engines spraying at the building, but not able to control the flames. I stood there in awe, until the firefighters created a perimeter for safety and asked me to move. I was right there watching it all go up in flames."

By the time word spread and the facts were known, the enormity of the loss sank in. The ruined product of more than seventy companies was calculated to be worth well over $100 million. Other clients such as C&H Sugar lost millions; film director Francis Ford Coppola lost tons of his signature pasta sauces and olive oils. The ravaging fire had started at 3:40 P.M. and hadn't been contained until 11:20 P.M.

A feeling of doom flooded her. She needed to go, but she couldn't just turn tail and skip the dinner.

"In the end, we lost the entire production of the 2003 vintage," says Delia. "Some $4.5 million worth of wine. It wasn't just the dollar amount. It was the work of more than twenty years, carving out a place in a restaurant's wine list, all the work in getting to those two hundred, three hundred, four hundred accounts, all of a sudden . . . gone." Many years later, there is still an edge in her voice while telling the story.

"That day marked a huge change in focus for the winery," Alan says. "We got together as a family and decided that we did not want to give up."

Janet was studying abroad, staying with family in Buenos Aires, when she heard the sad news. "I had to explain the situation to my aunts and uncles, who were also very worried," she says. "My mother's youngest brother, Christian, would become a source of moral support for her in the months to come."

Fortitude

THE PERPETRATOR was caught quickly. Facing embezzlement charges in Marin County, money problems, and eviction from the warehouse, investigators say the arsonist fired up a propane torch. He was burning evidence, according to Delia. He had been selling bottles of Bordeaux wine as "futures" to more people than appropriate, selling the same bottles several times. "It was a whole scam," she says. "And he thought that if he made it all disappear, insurance would cover it."

Prosecutor Steven Lapham, a wine lover himself, said, "He damaged so many lives. We tend to think of winery owners as being rich people, but by and large, the people storing wine at this facility were doing so because they didn't have their own storage. They were small wineries that couldn't afford these losses."

In the past, damaged wine had been sold with the labels still on the bottles—an illegal practice that could irreparably damage the reputation of a winery. So as soon as she could, Delia drove down to Mare Island. Because there was a certain amount of disorganization, she was able to enter the warehouse. The smell of soot and charred wine was overwhelming. Pallets of half-burnt bottles and cardboard boxes towered over her. She found what was left of her wine and funneled it out of the warehouse, to make sure no one would ever drink it.

"It was very bad timing," Delia says. "Very bad timing for me and for a number of people. And it was the typical insurance story: I had insurance, but the insurance company knows that they don't really need to pay you by tomorrow."

Indeed, VIADER would have zero wine for at least a year in an extremely competitive business. Neither did VIADER have bottles to give to those who had already paid for them. Yet Delia had to try to maintain the relationships she'd built up over the years, explaining to clients that it was a total loss, but to keep a spot open for her. "I would see them year after year, and they would just make fun of me," she says. "I didn't have bottled wine to sell, so I brought barrel samples to one big wine show with a little handmade label. I didn't have anything, but I needed to keep showing our wine so they would not forget.

"It almost put me out of business," she says. "I had so many demands. Nobody is going to put a placeholder on a restaurant's wine list if you don't have

Delia made sure that the bottles of boiled wine that actually survived the chaos of the Wines Central fire unbroken would never be drunk by anyone, and that meant VIADER was a winery with no wine to give to its customers.

wine to supply. They can't wait until you come out with the next vintage. And I still had to pay for the barrels and the bottles and the corks and everything else. I still had to pay for producing a wine that I didn't have for sale. Many other producers did not come back from that fire."

During the arsonist's trial, it was noted that several wineries closed, as did Wines Central itself. Ted Hall, whose Long Meadow Ranch Winery in St. Helena lost two vintages of Cabernet Sauvignon and its entire library of past vintages, gave an emotional speech, telling the court that this was more than just a property crime.

"My mother immediately went into crisis mode," Janet says. "It was a very difficult time, and possibly traumatic for my mother, because the winery provided for the livelihoods of over a dozen families who worked here. It weighed heavily on her that the business might not be able to afford to keep everybody employed."

Then, just as her twentieth harvest was about to end in 2006, her father was gravely ill. While Alan finished harvest and made the wine in consultation with Michel Rolland, Delia returned to Argentina to say goodbye to Walter, the one who had made it all possible.

Live Well
Laugh Often
Love Much

DIFFICULT TIMES: *(left and above)* The disastrous fire at Wines Central essentially forced Delia to start over from scratch, building up once again all the relationships she had spent the previous twenty years establishing. The following months and years saw a complete reshaping of the operation's business model, and it was the loyalty of VIADER's many fans that ultimately carried the day. • But if the crisis of the fire wasn't enough, Delia also had to find a way to move forward without one pillar of support she'd had all her life: her father, Walter Viader, passed away on October 21, 2006, at the age of eighty-five.

dear Delia
thank you for my new
billfold with money. I
shall spend it wisely
hope to see you soon

with love,
♡ Margot

FRIENDS AND COLLEAGUES: *(clockwise from top left)* Margrit Mondavi and Delia shared a special friendship. An avid artist, Margrit would adorn even the smallest notes with delightful hand-drawn pictures. • Naoko Dalla Valle, one of Delia's dearest friends, Naoko's sister, and Delia enjoy a dinner together at Charlie Trotter's in Chicago. • Delia smiles for a picture with her long-time friend Robert Mondavi. • Delia, Gina Gallo, David Freeman, Jean-Charles Boisset, Naoko Dalla Valle, Akiko Freeman, and Yumi Tanabe share a meal at The French Laundry in Yountville. • Margrit Mondavi and Delia had a bond that transcended work and wine.

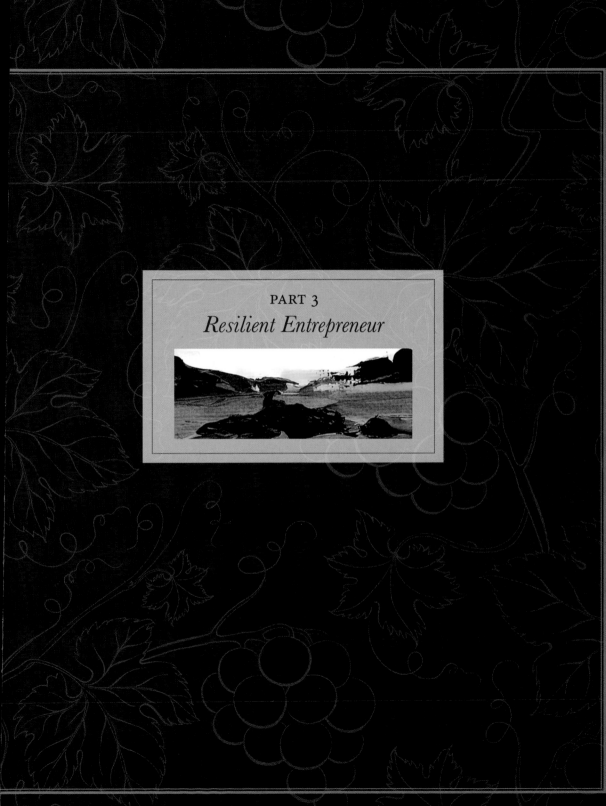

PART 3
Resilient Entrepreneur

Pivoting Gracefully

"I HAD TO START OVER, twenty years gone basically," Delia says. "Not only start over, I had to completely change our distribution strategy."

VIADER could no longer afford a global distribution model, exporting their wines to many countries. Instead, to obtain maximum revenue from each bottle, Delia would alter her business model and go directly to the consumer. That meant forming a kind of fan club and compiling mailing lists at a time when the nascent Internet trade of fine wine faced enormous legal barriers to shipping wine interstate.

"We had to learn a new and direct way of reaching our customers," Alan says. "There was very little wine available to sell. The only way for us to stay in business was to get full retail price. It transformed the business model entirely. We went from being over 50 percent sold in distribution before the fire and had to switch to over 95 percent sold direct to consumer, basically within months."

"I spoke to my most loyal distributor friends," Delia says, "and explained, 'This is a numbers game, and this is where our relationship will have to get on a trust footing, because you'll have to help me weather this. This is the plan, this is how I'm going to do it. This year you're not getting your entire allocation. Whatever wine I can allocate will be for the entire state, and those cases need to go to this account, this account, and this account. Nobody else.' And if they couldn't agree, because it didn't make financial sense to them, or for whatever other reason, then I just couldn't supply. I needed to do things differently after the fire."

In fact, VIADER once again began to use a more European model, effectively "what people in Bordeaux do," she says, "when they sell wine *en primeur*, which translates to wine sold while still on the vine." In other words, customers placed an order and paid in advance for wine they'd receive in three years' time. "I didn't have any wine to sell," she says. "And I needed to sell wine in order to pay the bills."

"We turned our focus to the next vintage and to our most loyal customers," Alan says. "I had to send out hundreds of handwritten letters explaining our situation and our commitment to the future of the family company. We opened up our personal library to them and sold our priceless history in bottles. We depleted practically the entire library inventory to help keep us in business."

"Mom was determined to do her best," Janet says. "And this led her to discover a new way to go to market: direct to consumer, which kept our company afloat."

Fortunately, VIADER found full support in countless loyal collectors worldwide.

After the 2005 warehouse fire wiped out all of VIADER's 2003 vintage, Delia had to sell her wine *en primeur*, or sold while still on the vine, which means loyal customers paid in advance for wine they would receive in three years' time.

The Next Generation

FOR A DECADE from 2001 to 2011, Delia and Alan experimented with biodynamics in the vineyard and the cellar, but the results did not prove to them that the increased cost was justified. "The soils were very alive but our vines were barely hanging in," Delia says.

They decided to balance organic farming with biodynamics. Today VIADER is Napa Green certified, indicating that the winery and its practices conserve natural resources and promote long-term sustainability. This is an important benchmark for both Delia and Alan.

Alan, for his part, was also helping to ensure the family's place in the winery's operation. For fifteen years, he had quite literally grown into the business. "Over time, I learned many techniques to hold my own in the vineyards," he says. "I'd

The winery's way forward is, and has always been, through the family. Alan oversees production of VIADER wines from start to finish, and Janet has taken up the mantle of keeping strong those business relationships that Delia nurtured for so many years.

worked side by side with the crews during pruning, leafing, and harvesting. I'd never liked to be given handouts or easy jobs, so I worked from the ground up and earned respect from the crew."

In 2007, Janet joined the VIADER company full time, embarking on her first trip to promote the family brand in New York City. "My mother has a sink-or-swim philosophy," Janet says, "and was confident that I could figure out my own sales techniques. Her advice was to pay attention to body language and to learn quickly how to 'read' people's reactions to my presentation. I was in my early twenties and very naive, although well informed and connected to our winemaking techniques and vineyard operations. Initially, these tough sommeliers underestimated me, probably in the same way they underestimated my mother when she first established the winery."

Delia's children have quite literally grown into the business.

The winery experienced another challenge when the financial crisis hit in 2008. "Making really good red wine takes a three-year cycle from harvest to bottle to market, so what comes three years after the fire of 2005? 2008," Delia sighs. "So here I am trying to get back up on my feet when 2008 happens."

In fact, the Wall Street meltdown had begun in 2007, and Delia's options came down to a choice between her Napa Valley home vineyard and winery and her burgeoning vineyard and home in Italy. She couldn't keep both. "You put years into something and it's not quite budding yet, and you have to let it go," she says. "At that moment, Bolgheri was just about to bear fruit, and you have to give it away and let somebody else enjoy the results of your hard work. I left the unborn child in a way, and that was a tremendous sadness."

Delia sold the vineyard property in Bolgheri through her Italian partners, and then she had to sell her house in San Vincenzo. And with it went Delia's dream of an Italian retirement.

Still, it was another crisis averted, another occasion to display quick thinking coupled with the discipline and adaptability to execute, traits that had served Delia throughout her life. "If I can't go this way, maybe I will go that way, but I'll get there because I'm confident of the outcome. It's a combination of focus and optimism that perhaps you could call grit—the belief that success isn't always a straight and easy shot from here to there. My family is what helps me stay focused."

THE LONDON WINE MAN

Donald Kurtz, Chairman of the Board

December 4, 2000

TO: **DELIA VIADER**

FROM: **DONALD KURTZ and DOUG COHEN**

Dear Delia

Look at it this way: not only did you outrank everyone in the new world, losing only to someone who probably had a century's head start on you in making wine, but you also outranked every single Bordeaux in existence. Including Margaux, Petrus, Latour, Lafite, Mouton, Cheval Blanc, Ausone, Haut Brion and all the rest of those pretenders.

I'd say that was a pretty good showing.

Congratulations again. It was great!

Best regards

Donald
Doug

THE LONDON WINE MAN INC 8326-J Arrowridge Boulevard

ALAN K. SIMPSON

United States Senator (Ret.)
WYOMING

June 21, 2006

Delia Viader
PO Box 280
Deer Park, CA 94576

Dear Delia:

Aren't you the thoughtful one!? Thank you so much for the six bottles of the rare Napa Cabernet Franc. Now that truly is the gift that keeps on giving! You were very thoughtful and kind to do that, and Ann and I are deeply appreciative.

We are so pleased that you enjoyed your time at the unique Alfalfa activities. It is all such fun and so hard to describe to people who have not participated. It was a delight to share some of that time with you.

Meanwhile, thank you again for your generosity and kindness. Take care, be well and Ann joins in sending fond regards to you and all of your dear ones.

CHEZ PANISSE RESTAURANT & CAFÉ
1517 Shattuck Avenue Berkeley, California 94709

6·20·07.

Dear Delia,
It was so wonderful
to come to you high
vineyards from the
Davos Brainstorming!
Thank you for allowing
us to make ourselves
at home with the
cooking. Sincerely
Alice Waters

ACCOLADES: *(left to right)* A colleague acknowledges VIADER's well-deserved #2 ranking in the 2001 *Wine Spectator* Top 100. • Letter to Delia from former US Senator Alan Simpson, on the occasion of Sandra Day O'Connor's retirement from the Supreme Court. • Famous Bay Area chef Alice Waters, owner of Chez Panisse in Berkeley, sent a thank-you note following a three-day event that VIADER hosted for a Davos World Economic Forum brainstorming session, with the *Harvard Business Review* acting as moderator. The highly secretive and ultraexclusive think tank event was attended by a group of influential world business executives.

A Family Business

IF YOU WERE TO VISIT VIADER winery, you'd find a bustling center of activity: guests tasting different wines, vineyard crews going about their tasks, Delia and her grown children at work. In the main cellar, you'd also see proudly displayed the flag of "Free Catalonia," something that no doubt would have pleased Delia's grandfather.

More observant visitors might note small Asian statues scattered between the trees, the water fountains, and the moss-covered rocks with unique shapes used in the building of the tasting room, offices, planters, and walls, carefully collected from the land surrounding the vineyards. They would delight in the eight different types of flowering lavender and the estate's thoughtfully preserved natural landscape, designed to attract bees and contribute to the aromatics of VIADER wines.

"I'm happy because we're so small that I get to know all of our wine club members on a first-name basis," Delia says, "and I've actually become friends with most of them. But I do also miss Europe. I miss having the opportunity to present my wines in places where I got to know the chef or owner."

Over the years, the winery's offerings have grown: VIADER, a blend of Cabernet Sauvignon and Cabernet Franc nicknamed "Liquid Cashmere"; VIADER, "V" a blend of Cabernet Sauvignon and Petit Verdot; VIADER "Black Label" Estate Limited Edition, a unique blend of Syrah, Cabernet Sauvignon, and Cabernet Franc with a pinch of Malbec added, "just like that 'pinch' of salt that makes a dish stand out," says Alan; and DARE by VIADER, highlighting the attributes of a single varietal, Cabernet Franc, to enjoy upon release as an everyday wine to accompany a meal.

"Delia's wine choices are daring," Jo Diaz wrote in her *Wine Blog*. "This is a woman of the world. She made her choice to not craft a regional wine. She decided to take on the world . . . in the most quiet, elegantly humble way

Delia Viader today—the same visionary, resilient leader, philosopher, mother, and innovator she was three decades ago when she defied all odds to build a vineyard on the impossibly steep, rocky slopes of Howell Mountain.

possible. . . . It's that posture that's made her a giant, who still understands that she's just a blink in time . . . like the rest of us."

"It wasn't until I started working in the cellar full-time that my mom formally invited me to participate in the wine-blending sessions," Alan says. "I didn't have a vote yet, but it was fascinating to follow the process and to learn from my mom how our wines were created. Before that, I didn't fully connect the vineyard practices to the final wines. It was a very detailed education on the correlation that exists between the vines, the place, the soil, and the final wine. I learned that everything is connected. Today, I work on the final blends together with my mother. We make sure nothing is put into a bottle that we both don't love."

WINE FAMILY: *(clockwise from top left)* Delia with her daughter-in-law Mariela and first grandchild, Matthew Alan. • Janet, Alan, and Alex being pulled into a hug. • Delia started her winery with her family in mind—*(left to right)* pictured here in 2017 are Paul, Matthew, Delia, Alan, Elizabeth Grace (Lizzy), Mariela, Janet, and Jonathan Robert (Jony). • Delia's close-knit family enjoys their time together—*(left to right)* Paul, Alex, Janet, Mariela, Delia, and Alan.

INTERNATIONAL EVENTS: *(clockwise from top left)* Outside the Hotel InterContinental in Tokyo, Japan, Delia poses with colleagues from an international wine event. • Delia, attending one of the Vinexpos in Bordeaux, France, in the 1990s. Pictured behind her is Michela Rodeno, the general manger for St. Supéry Estate Vineyards at that time. • Delia, along with Napa Valley Vintners, put on a very exclusive tasting event at the American Embassy in London, 2002. • VIADER wines are featured at a wine event in Montreal. • Delia and colleagues at an event in Tokyo.

Legacy

"I'M NOT SURE whether I chose wine or wine chose me," Delia explains. "But it's something that is very, very much alive in me, in as much as I put a lot of me into that bottle. It's the part of winemaking that I enjoy the most; blending and creating . . . nurturing.

"My vision for our family legacy existed before I had even harvested my first grapes. Once we finally started construction of the winery and wine caves, I began outlining a family succession plan. As a single mother and sole provider, I was determined to have everything set in place. In retrospect, the situation caused by the fire brought us so much closer, now with four members of the family working together."

As planned, Delia's business enabled her to raise her children, send them to college, and help them out with their first cars and their first homes. Today, Alan's main responsibilities are vineyard management and winemaking, but because it's a small property, he wears many hats; walking the vineyards and talking to everyone on the team to make sure things are running smoothly. "I'm usually the guy people call when something breaks or if a tree falls over the driveway," he says.

Alan plans improvements, organizes and schedules crews for day-to-day operations, works with his mother on an administrative level and on strategy and future projections, and above all, he maintains quality. "I try to help make our wines even better in the cellar year after year," he says. "From harvest pick decisions to pump over schedules to racking and blending trials, I have the responsibility of making that happen."

To hone his skills, Alan attends seminars and workshops, always on the lookout for useful techniques and technology. His wife, Mariela, a professionally trained chef, is also VIADER's executive chef and is the hand behind the chocolate

---

On any given day, one can stand on the porch of the VIADER tasting room, looking out over the family-tended vineyards below, and recognize the story of passion, dedication, and love.

The Viaders stand on the well-trodden road in front of the winery—*(left to right)* the family dog, Delia, Jony, Janet, Mateo, Mariela, and Alan.

bark offered at VIADER's tastings. As such, she prepares dishes, often gathered from the estate's organic garden, to pair with their wines at private events and educational wine tastings, either at home or across the country. Alan likes to cook, too—whole lambs, "the Argentine way, over an open-spit fire. We are a family-owned winery," he says, "and we help each other out as needed."

Together, Mariela and Alan are initiating their three children, Delia's grandchildren, into the wine business, letting them participate, from riding with Papa on the forklift around the cellar to tasting the grapes right before harvest. "Built-in quality control," Alan jokes. "But I'm also looking at the distant future, having my children help me, much like I helped my mother. My boys have already experienced harvest since they were infants. They help shift the bin-dumper; they've done berry sampling with me since the time that they could walk. I'm trying to expose them to grape growing as much as my mother did for me. They already know how wine is made and are eager to help their Papa at work any chance they get. It's fun and exciting for them, and I look forward to watching them grow, and perhaps someday they'll take the winery even further, beyond my expectations."

For her part, Janet has followed in her mother's footsteps, studying in Paris, but at the even more prestigious Sciences Po university through the University of California–Berkeley's study abroad program. Janet is also, with Alan, part of "NG: Next Generation in Wine," a collaborative marketing group of second-generation wine growers. She also served as one of the youngest elected members on the Board of Directors of the Napa Valley Vintners Association.

"My brother Alan is dedicated to maintaining and improving the quality standards of our vineyard and winemaking," says Janet. "I strive for developing authentic connections with our customers and to always be an ambassador for our family's wine brand."

"That's the beauty of the wine business—family and traditions preserved for the next generation; in a way, a *legacy*," says Delia. "Something you created and cherished all your life that you can pass on to the next generation.

"As my dearest friend Margrit Mondavi would sagely advise: 'Always have something to look forward to.' I look forward to seeing my children continue on, for their children's sake and their children's children.

"To them and the generations to come, I dedicate the following poem."

"*If—*"

BY RUDYARD KIPLING

If you can keep your head when all about you
Are losing theirs and blaming it on you,
If you can trust yourself when all men doubt you,
But make allowance for their doubting too;
If you can wait and not be tired by waiting,
Or being lied about, don't deal in lies,
Or being hated, don't give way to hating,
And yet don't look too good, nor talk too wise:

If you can dream—and not make dreams your master;
If you can think—and not make thoughts your aim;
If you can meet with Triumph and Disaster
And treat those two impostors just the same;
If you can bear to hear the truth you've spoken
Twisted by knaves to make a trap for fools,
Or watch the things you gave your life to, broken,
And stoop and build 'em up with worn-out tools:

If you can make one heap of all your winnings
And risk it on one turn of pitch-and-toss,
And lose, and start again at your beginnings
And never breathe a word about your loss;
If you can force your heart and nerve and sinew
To serve your turn long after they are gone,
And so hold on when there is nothing in you
Except the Will which says to them: "Hold on!"

If you can talk with crowds and keep your virtue,
Or walk with Kings—nor lose the common touch,
If neither foes nor loving friends can hurt you,
If all men count with you, but none too much;
If you can fill the unforgiving minute
With sixty seconds' worth of distance run,
Yours is the Earth and everything that's in it,
And—which is more—you'll be a Man, my son!

Painted with VIADER
NAPA VALLEY 2000
Philippe DUFRENOY.

Bordelais artist Philippe Dufrenoy, the man who paints with wine, created this portrait of Delia with
VIADER Napa Valley 2000.

La meva terra, Catalunya
La meva parla, el català
La meva dansa, la sardana
El meu desig, La llibertat.

A Cry for Freedom

DELIA'S CATALAN HERITAGE has always been close to her heart. Sitting on her grandfather's knee, playing a game in which she proclaimed herself "Catalan! and Free!" is one of her most enduring memories from childhood.

For the uninitiated, Barcelona, Catalonia's capital, is simply a tourist attraction best known for tapas, its world-class soccer team, and the works of Antoni Gaudí, the architect of the Sagrada Família cathedral. Many Catalans have grown to adulthood believing that they were simply *not Spanish*. Under Generalissimo Francisco Franco's dictatorship, which lasted three decades and ended in 1975, the government tried to stamp out all Catalan institutions, as well as the language, and thousands of people were executed in purges. No Catalan family emerged from that period unscathed. Now Catalan freedom is once again finding a way into Delia's life, as the world watches with interest Catalonia's October 1, 2017 voting and subsequent declaration of independence. Ask *independistas* why the need to break away from Spain is so urgent, and the answer goes back to 1714, when Philip V of Spain captured Barcelona during the war of the Spanish Succession, bringing an end to the Catalan principality. In Catalonia, this is not obscure history—it is common these days to hear the archaic insult *botifler*, which means a supporter of Philip V and his ally, the French House of Bourbon. Delia's own grandfather, Joan Pedro Rafael Viader, was among those who lost everything he had in his homeland of Catalonia when Franco took power. The October 1 vote was regarded as illegal by the Spanish government, and many of the leaders of Catalonia's pro-independence movement, including regional president Carles Puigdemont, have been charged with crimes against the state. Now Puigdemont is in exile, Spain and the international community still do not recognize Catalonia's declaration of independence, and the Catalan people are in deadlock with the rest of their legal country. We will have to wait to see how this all plays out.

LEFT: Catalans protest in Barcelona, 2017. ABOVE: This plate summarizes well the spirit "My land is Catalonia; My language is Catalan; My dance is la Sardana; My desire: Liberty."

Epilogue

"I LOVE PEOPLE, and I love meeting people," Delia says. "Sharing a glass of wine surrounded by family and friends at the table breeds conviviality. For all I have accomplished, I also look forward to the many more things that I would like to do. I'd like to keep exploring and discovering new places and new cultures and new wines."

Back home, her once-small ficus, the tree in her living room planter, has grown to over twenty feet tall. "Sometimes I feel like I've crammed eight or nine lives into one. I would like to imagine a bottle of my wine being enjoyed perhaps ten or twenty years from now. I might not be there, but I will still be making people happy."

The vision of her family taking over her creation remains constant. "Adding their vision onto mine, and then passing it on to their children . . . I look forward to seeing my kids take this cherished little piece of heaven, and move forward, taking what I created as their own creation and in time, in their own ways, moving forward."

Asked about his vision, Alan says, "I'm still growing into it. I'm learning something new every day. My mother has built an amazing foundation for this company, and I would like to keep it in the family and take it to the next level. I've spent the last sixteen years making improvements to our vineyards, and as they continue to mature, I see only better and better quality coming from them. I'm also making adjustments to our cellar practices, purchasing new equipment, taking advantage of newer and better technologies. These are exciting times, with so many great vintages coming from this property."

"We will continue to create beautiful wines," says Janet, "and to cultivate experiences in line with our reputation for consistent quality. I see us remaining small in size and production. Our family will always be very hands-on because that is part of what defines us. Family owned and operated. Working together as a team in something we are all passionate about."

When asked about what she wanted in this celebratory album, Delia replied, "A story. Just tell my story. I would like to present it with a special bottling

commemorating our first thirty years, all bound together in a special package—
friends will hopefully enjoy the story and the wine, and perhaps share many
other good stories of their own."

Notice to customers as it reads on our tasting room's wall plaque:
This bright new day, complete with 24 hours of opportunities, choices, and attitudes.
A perfectly matched set of 1,440 minutes. This unique gift, this one day, cannot be
exchanged, replaced, or refunded. Handle with Care. Make the most of it. There is
only one to a customer.

BEAUTIFUL FAMILY, BEAUTIFUL WINES: Delia and her son Paul share a moment at the winery. •
(following spread) The VIADER tasting room is nestled in the trees of Howell Mountain.

Appendix

Bibliography

Dinkelspiel, Frances. *Tangled Vines: Greed, Murder, Obsession, and an Arsonist in the Vineyards of California.* New York: St. Martin's Press, 2015.

Heintz, William. *California's Napa Valley: One Hundred Sixty Years of Wine Making.* San Francisco: Scottwall Associates, 1999.

"How Morley Safer Convinced Americans to Drink More Wine." *60 Minutes Overtime*, August 28, 2016. https://www.cbsnews.com/news/how-morley-safer-convinced-americans-to-drink-more-wine/.

"Judgment of Paris." Wikipedia. https://en.wikipedia.org/wiki/Judgment_of_Paris_(wine).

Lukacs, Paul. *American Vintage: The Rise of American Wine.* Boston: Houghton Mifflin, 2000.

Mendelson, Richard. *Appellation Napa Valley: Building and Protecting an American Treasure.* Napa, CA: Val de Grace Books, 2016.

Pinney, Thomas. *A History of Wine in America: From the Beginnings to Prohibition.* Berkeley: UC Press, 1989.

Sullivan, Charles L. *Napa Wine: A History from Mission Days to Present.* 2nd ed. San Francisco: Wine Appreciation Guild, 2008.

SOURCES

Americanleasing.com
Berkeleyside.com
JamesSuckling.com
Napagreen.org
Napavalleyregister.com

Rombauer.com
Sfgate.com
TheWineCellarInsider.com
Wine-blog.org

Winemag.com
Winesandvines.com

Acknowledgments

Delia would like to thank the following people, without whom this book would not have been possible: Jonathon Rinzler; Richard Mendelson; Chris Gruener, Iain Morris, Suzi Hutsell, Jan Hughes, and Mason Harper at Cameron + Co; photographers Jason Lang, Luisa Bonachea, Cathy O'Hagain, and Bradley Gray; and her family, Alan and Mariela Viader, Janet Viader, Paul Viader, Alex Viader, and Herb Beard. A very special thank you to VIADER's Wine Club members, for whom this book was made.

Contributors

J. W. RINZLER, former executive editor at Lucasfilm Ltd., is the author of the *New York Times* bestseller *The Making of Star Wars* and *London Times* bestseller *The Complete Making of Indiana Jones*, as well as a #1 *New York Times* bestselling graphic novel adapted from George Lucas's original rough draft of "The Star Wars." He lives on the northern California coast.

RICHARD MENDELSON, a native Floridian, went to Harvard and then fell in love with wine while doing post-graduate work at Oxford. From there, he immersed himself in a yearlong apprenticeship at one of the most prestigious wineries in Burgundy. Mendelson earned his law degree from Stanford Law School and headed for what was the exciting new frontier of American wine and food: the Napa Valley. His previous books include *From Demon to Darling: A Legal History of Wine in America*; *Wine in America: Law and Policy*; and *Spirit in Metal*, about his work in metal sculptures. Richard and his wife, Marilyn, live in Napa, California.

VIADER®

NAPA VALLEY

Viader Vineyards & Winery
1120 Deer Park Road
Deer Park, CA 94576
www.viader.com

Text copyright © 2018 Viader Vineyards & Winery
Photographs copyright © 2018 Viader Vineyards & Winery, unless otherwise noted.

Page 13 Courtesy of Library of Congress, Geography and Map Division; 79, 157, 164
© Jason Lang; 93 (top and bottom right) © Luisa Bonachea; 105 © Cathy O'Hagain; 126, 127
© *Wine Spectator*; 143 © 2005 Bradley Gray; 144 © 2005 Bureau of Alcohol, Tobacco, Firearms
and Explosives; 167 © Philippe Dufrenoy; 168 © MarcoPachiega / Shutterstock.com

ISBN: 978-1-944903-53-4

10   9   8   7   6   5   4   3   2   1

Manufactured in China

CAMERON + COMPANY
149 Kentucky Street, Suite 7
Petaluma, CA 94952
www.cameronbooks.com

Publisher: *Chris Gruener*
Creative Director: *Iain R. Morris*
Designer: *Suzi Hutsell*
Managing Editor: *Jan Hughes*
Editorial Assistant: *Mason Harper*

DELIA VIADER's journey to success can be characterized by her fortitude. A tireless visionary, Delia is an Argentine who speaks six languages, received a PhD in philosophy, raised four children alone in a new country, acquired land, constructed houses—and built a world-class, award-winning winery on the impossibly rocky slopes of Howell Mountain in Napa Valley. Hers is a story of passion, tenacity, and acumen. Literally having to drill through the rocks to create holes for the vine roots to take hold, Viader Vineyards and Winery is now a leading first-growth wine estate. Nurturing her vines, her business, and her children, Delia's lasting legacy was born of strength of character and a commitment to family and community.

CAMERON + COMPANY

149 KENTUCKY, SUITE 7, PETALUMA, CA, 94952
(707) 769-1617 • WWW.CAMERONBOOKS.COM

PRINTED IN CHINA

ISBN: 978-1-944903-53-4 | US $25.00

52500

9 781944 903534